P9-AOL-503

SOVIET ECONOMIC DEVELOPMENT:

Operation Outstrip, 1921-1965

ANATOLE G. MAZOUR

Professor of History, Emeritus
Stanford University

AN ANVIL ORIGINAL

under the general editorship of

LOUIS L. SNYDER

D. VAN NOSTRAND COMPANY, INC.

PRINCETON, NEW JERSEY

TORONTO   LONDON

VAN NOSTRAND REGIONAL OFFICES
New York, Chicago, San Francisco

D. VAN NOSTRAND COMPANY, LTD., *London*

D. VAN NOSTRAND COMPANY (Canada), LTD., *Toronto*

HC
335
.M412

PREFACE

In dealing with the economic development of the Soviet Union since 1917, particularly in a brief comparative account, one is bound to face an abundance of evidence much of which can hardly be discussed in any measurable terms. Using Western yardsticks of estimating costs and return to analyze Soviet economic growth is not always realistic because many necessary factors are often either not available or are extremely elusive. Can one make an accurate estimate of the cost of the bitter struggle with the peasantry during the period of War Communism or with the Kulak elements during the thirties? What measure is one to apply in estimating the cost of violence during the rule of Stalin, the purges of managerial talent, the forced-labor methods, the repressive labor laws, with all the sociological implications these must undoubtedly have had? Equally elusive is the value of services the citizen receives in the Soviet Union that are unavailable or prohibitively costly elsewhere.

In 1965, for the first time since 1937, the Soviet government published precise figures, instead of just percentages, on the average pay of Soviet workers, which comes to approximately 60 cents (54 kopeks) an hour. This places the Soviet worker behind the Israeli, who earns on an average 63 cents per hour, and ahead of the Argentinian and Mexican, who earn 58 and 56 cents respectively. Such comparisons, however, are deceptive, since these do not take into account the purchase power of wages. Furthermore, while some national yearbooks, citing statistical data on wages, include fringe benefits, others do not. At best, therefore, statistical comparisons have dubious meaning; at worst, they can lead to misinterpretations and erroneous impressions.

3

A study of Soviet economic development demands complete fairness and impartiality. The devastating price the Russian people have paid for their economic progress must be reckoned in terms of both the tangible and intangible factors. The student must consider both the debit and credit side of the balance sheet regardless of his personal feelings.

Economic advancement must objectively and carefully be examined in terms of the social goals of the society. Has Soviet society gained more from the abolition of economic inequality or would it have gained more without going through the convulsions of communism and ending with Libermanism? Or, what is more sound, an economy based on private monopoly or one based on state monopoly? What is preferable, a system of economic security without affluence, or economic insecurity in an affluent society? What is better, a society that tolerates social parasitism, inequity through inheritance, and appalling waste, or a social order that believes in physical elimination of the idle and suppresses inequity and private control of means of production?

How is one able to put a price on individual freedom? What effects do restrictions on personal freedom have upon the individual's creative gifts, upon his initiative in commerce, trade, social, or political activities? At the same time it is possible to calculate the stifling impact of the fantastic growth of the bureaucratic machine, so aptly pointed out by Milovan Djilas in his *The New Class*. (*See Reading No. 23.*) And what about the forced isolation into which the nation has been placed in the field of economic development?

Since this is mainly an economic study, it is necessary to put aside such questions as other impacts, sociological, cultural, or moral—subjects too complex to deal with. Yet they should not be overlooked.

If the brevity of this study imposes only mere mention of the main aspects of its topic, the author hopes that even their casual mention may lead to a deeper insight into the problems involved, in which case author's labor will have been highly rewarded.

The author is deeply indebted to Theodore Shabad, Moscow correspondent of *The New York Times,* for his generous permission to utilize his superb dispatches. These, as well as the material in the monthly journal *Soviet Geography* of which Mr. Shabad is editor, have proved indispensable for the study of current economic developments in the Soviet Union.

The following periodical and newspapers have proved indispensable as sources of information and have been utilized extensively: *The Economist* (London), *The New York Times, The New York Herald Tribune.*

Some parts of this study have originally appeared in an earlier work by the present author under the title of *Russia, Tsarist and Communist.*

A. G. M.

TABLE OF CONTENTS

PART II—READINGS

Part I

OPERATION OUTSTRIP:
SOVIET ECONOMIC DEVELOPMENT

— 1 —

AN EXPERIMENT IN
WAR COMMUNISM

Nationalization of Industry. When in November 1917 the Bolsheviks unseated the Provisional Government and established themselves in power, the economic affairs of Russia were already at a low ebb. The war years and early months of the revolution were a serious drain on the economy of the nation. National production was rapidly declining while an increased scarcity of vital commodities brought a ravaging black market. The inflationary currency decreased daily in value and added further confusion and chaos to the general state of economic affairs. Skilled labor gradually was dissipated, laborers moving from urban to rural communities in the hope of improving opportunities for subsistence. Transport was rapidly reaching a state of complete breakdown; there was widespread demoralization of the railway personnel, while the wear and tear of rolling stock led to a virtual standstill of many lines. Engines and cars remained idle, passenger cars became rare, and shops were deserted. The railroads, which were never noted for their profitable management, came to face staggering deficits. Many vital industries, aside from increased skilled labor shortages, were additionally handicapped by shortages of raw materials. It was in the midst of such developments that the recently formed Soviet government launched its program of nationalization of all resources and plunged the nation into an experiment of War Communism. By so doing the government committed itself to abolishing economic inequity once and for all. In one of its first decrees of

November 13, 1917, the Council of People's Commissars
(Sovnarkom) announced a policy of social insurance for
all workers and "city and village poor." (*See Reading No.
1.*) Shortly after, the Central Executive Committee decreed
banking a state monopoly and all banks nationalized. (*See
Reading No. 2.*) On February 16, 1918, the Supreme
Council announced regulations which defined further the
policy concerning confiscated industrial enterprises. (*See
Reading No. 3.*) A week later the Soviet of People's
Commissars nationalized all foreign trade. (*See Reading
No. 4.*)

Official abolition of inequity and all the acts of property nationalization did not relieve the desperate state
in which the national economy found itself. There was
little produced and less to distribute. No one had realized
the sorrowful state of affairs more than Lenin did. But
Lenin, carried on the crest of the revolution as the rest,
felt concession to capitalism in any form would have be-
trayed the socialist faith and imperiled the entire cause.
It took another three years of experience before he was
ready for retreat. The initial policy of a strict application
of a socialized economy therefore was doggedly pursued.

A decree of April 27, 1918, abolished inheritance
by law or testament and declared all property of decedent
in excess of 10,000 rubles to be state owned. (*See Reading No. 5.*) At the same time the government took over
outrightly from the factory committees all plants and
factories. The corresponding growth of the administrative
bureaucracy in all enterprises, accompanied by inexperi-
ence, mismanagement, confusion, and chaos, produced in
the end a further decline in production and an increase
in inefficiency.

By the end of June 1918 the government had taken
another major step when most industrial and commercial
enterprises, "with all their capital and property," became
the property of the Soviet state, affecting 1,100 joint-
stock companies with a total capital of about 3 million
rubles. (*See Reading No. 6.*) This act included all important mines, factories, and mills, placing these within
the jurisdiction of the Supreme Council of National Economy. All administrative officers of the affected industrial

enterprises were ordered to remain at their posts; their departure, it was declared, would be regarded as criminal negligence and prosecuted accordingly. Simultaneously all private capital was frozen, pending further action.

Along with these sweeping decrees a Joint Conference of Factory-Shop Committees and Trade Unions virtually outlawed strikes, demanded labor discipline, and called for concentrated effort to end the prevailing economic chaos. Any form of work stoppage was outlawed, and those responsible for inciting labor unrest were to be dealt with by special courts.

In August 1918 a decree issued by the Central Executive Committee abolished the ownership of real estate. (*See Reading No. 7.*) The right to own land or buildings in cities was abolished, and all mortgages of more than 10,000 rubles were annulled. Mortgages of less than 10,000 rubles became state loans.

Labor, Production, and Distribution. Responsibility for production, and consequently for distribution, was henceforth to rest upon the government. The Constitution of July 10, 1918, adopted by the Fifth All-Russian Congress of Soviets, abolished "all exploitation of man by man," abolished "division of society into classes," socialized all land and resources, and confirmed the establishment of a "Workers' Control" and a "Supreme Council of National Economy." (Article 3, Clause C.) (*See Reading No. 8.*) The Supreme Council of National Economy was given the authority to manage the nationalized industry. The Council was granted broad powers and entrusted with the coordination of both national production and distribution. Various industrial branches were soon consolidated, forming trusts, each administered separately.

At the same time, independent commissariats were established dealing with such areas as Trade, Industry, Agriculture, and Finance. Since these Programs were hastily carried through, authority was not always defined or delineated clearly; many functions overlapped and authority was duplicated. Early in September 1918 labor discipline was further tightened: the Labor Commissariat announced that no unemployed worker had the right to refuse temporary work or to refuse to be transferred for work elsewhere. By the end of October another decree proclaimed all citizens, with a few exceptions, subject to compulsory labor.

Nationalization of all means of production led to government-controlled distribution, which proved an even more difficult and complex undertaking. Two agencies were used to plan for proper distribution in a socialist society, the Commissariat of Food and the Commissariat of Agriculture. These were assigned the task of provisioning the population with articles of mass consumption.

Lenin himself must have had many misgivings about too hasty action. He was approached on various occasions by labor representatives who demanded actions against factory owners. To these Lenin had one answer, that he was ready to sign at any time an act of nationalizing industry. But then he significantly hastened to inquire whether the workers were familiar with administrative problems, with industrial management; whether they knew something about methods of production, and about domestic and foreign trade related to the production involved. The answer was invariably negative.

Setting up machinery for distribution was only one part of the problem. The major difficulty was the location of foodstuffs and articles to be distributed. Here, despite all measures undertaken with "revolutionary determination," despite all fulminations and intimidations, little was found to satisfy the starving nation. Drastic rationing was soon introduced, requisitioning became widespread, violators of recently promulgated laws were brutally penalized, and still none or only small amounts of the sought commodities were to be found to replenish the empty warehouses. Rationing in its severest form became necessary. The Commissariat of Supplies (*Narkomprod*), in a spirit of true "revolutionary justice," and to utilize the little that was available, divided the population into four categories: (1) workers performing exceptionally hard and hazardous manual labor; (2) workers in other industries; (3) the rapidly growing ranks of government employees; and (4) the parasitic "nontoiling" citizens. Each group was entitled to a proportionately smaller daily ration of food and other hard to find consumer commodities. If the first three often had to subsist on less than a starving minimum, the fourth category could only expect manna from heaven.

War Communism. The formation of the White armies with foreign support and the beginning of the Civil War threw the country into total chaos. Whatever effort had been channeled into the restoration of normal life in the country was now disrupted; valuable economic areas were cut off from the center, depriving the government both of foodstuffs and of industrial resources. The desperate efforts of the government to hold the power it recently seized and to have the state overcome the resulting shortages resulted in a policy commonly known as War Communism. Partly ideology and partly emergency policies combined to shape this desperate effort into the notorious pattern that makes the period stand out in the history of the Revolution. With virtually no functioning monetary system the government was forced to follow a policy of barter and payments in kind. Eventually many services were granted free, including housing, utilities, and public transportation. There was speculation about total abolition of taxes and even money itself. Some enthusiasts regarded the policy of War Communism as only a preliminary step toward the realization of a true communist society. Yet Lenin himself was forced to admit that War Communism as a policy was forced upon the government "by war and ruin . . . as a temporary measure."

In the towns and cities War Communism received mixed support. It was enthusiastically supported by the leftist members of the party, lukewarmly upheld by the rightists, but only grudgingly accepted by most people. There was another story in the countryside. The peasantry hated it and violently opposed communism in whatever shape or form. They refused to yield their produce, contributing heavily to the acute shortage of foodstuffs. They would cut their sowing area; they would bury whatever they did produce, or destroy any surplus grain if need be; they would sell illegally on the black market, but they would not surrender it to the government. The black market flourished regardless of all the measures undertaken to suppress it. Regardless of all hazards, hungry consumers carried their worldly possessions to the market, hoping to exchange these for whatever available produce they might find on the black market.

City versus Country. As months passed by, the crisis became more acute, and more stringent measures were applied to crush peasant opposition. The government began to dispatch special contingents of troops, who mercilessly requisitioned all grain they were able to locate and carried out punitive missions. And still the peasants refused to alter their position: they continued to produce barely enough for their own subsistence and remained totally indifferent to the appeals from the cities to "save the fate of the revolution." As far as the peasant was concerned the land taken over and claimed by him marked the triumph of the revolution, and the verdict of history was irreversible.

From this brutal struggle with the rebellious peasantry the government derived many hard-learned lessons. One of these was that parceling out land in small strips among the peasants contributed little to the revolution and proved no economic solution to the state. The outcome was an armed peasantry controlling the land, inadvertently possessing a powerful economic weapon with which it was able to threaten the government, the city, the revolution itself. The irony of the situation was that the former revolutionary battle cry—Land to the Peasant!— seemed to have turned into a deadly weapon against the revolution. Small wonder the exasperated government came to regard the situation as being totally intolerable. It was determined, at whatever cost, to liberate itself and the city from the economic dependence upon the non-cooperative hostile peasantry.

Already in July 1918 a resolution was adopted by the Congress of Soviets which called for a consolidation of agricultural communes and state farms. It aimed to bring closer cooperation between town and country by introducing large-scale socialized agriculture. A policy of such scope, naturally, implied considerable government control, investment capital, and much opposition in the villages.

On August 3, 1918, the Commissariat of Agriculture issued a decree which may be regarded as the basis of the Soviet agrarian policy aiming at an overall socialized method of agriculture. The law that soon followed, promulgated on February 14, 1919, was a logical sequence to the initial steps toward socialized agriculture. Entitled "Regulations Concerning the Socialist Organization of the Land Measures for Facilitating the Introduction of the Socialist System of Agriculture," the law meant precisely that. The new legislation, the government firmly believed, was bound to raise the standards of scientific cultivation; it would be instrumental in improving relations between the proletariat of the city and the peasantry of the countryside; it would also aid in raising the general cultural level throughout the country.

The management of the state farms was entrusted to the Supreme Council of National Economy. The project, though highly ambitious and holding out the promise of solving the food problem, remained in reality largely a paper scheme. A combination of reasons may explain its failure. Partly it was due to the preoccupation of the government with the war effort. In part it can be attributed to the effective stubborn opposition of the peasantry to any form of socialization. The relentless struggle continued and at times assumed the character of open warfare between city and countryside. The blockade and foreign intervention aggravated matters further.

A Summary of the First Test of Power. The three-year civil war brought the country to the brink of a complete national catastrophe. Chaos, material destruction, and appalling misery prevailed throughout the land. The ferocity with which the various forces contended for political power left a trail of desolation rarely paralleled in history. To the ravages of the civil strife and War Communism may be added the foreign blockade which contributed no small share to the undermining and collapse of the national economy. By 1921 industrial production had dropped to some 13 percent of the pre-1914 level, while agriculture—the very backbone of the country's economy—was in total chaos. The peasants' aversion to any form of socialized agriculture led the country to the lowest level of subsistence. Transportation was at a virtual standstill. The nation seemed to have been held together by universal destitution. When by the end of 1921 the Russian people began to take stock after seven

years of war, revolution, and, finally, an unprecedented
drought and famine, the immediate question was not an
ideological one, but a problem of sheer physical survival.

In the center of all the difficulties stood the old issue—
the peasant. The land decree of the Bolsheviks legalized
the confiscation of all the landlords' estates. This land
was to be equally divided among the peasants. In a strict
sense this was merely the sanctioning of an act already
carried out by the peasants. Furthermore, by so doing the
government in fact recognized a nation of peasant small-
holders. Unwittingly it had therefore rendered a stamp
of approval to the creation of the peculiar dichotomy—a
bourgeois setting in the countryside versus communist
authority in urban communities. The entire situation was
fraught with conflict within party ranks as well as between
city and country.

Having gained control over the land that formerly belonged to the state or the gentry, the peasantry soon came
into sharp conflict with the government. Desperately
pressed by war conditions and motivated by party ideology the government adopted a policy known as War
Communism. Accordingly, village communities remained
in control of the land, but the state made every effort to
control the produce of the land. Individual tillers were
allowed small plots to produce enough for subsistence
while the rest was hopefully expected to be yielded to the
state. This the peasant resented with remarkable parochial
obstinacy: he refused to till the land for the pittance he
was permitted to retain or for the valueless paper currency
in which he was paid. The great issues of the revolution
were beyond his grasp—he had no faith in the socialist
kingdom of heaven. As long as the city had nothing to
offer him in return for his labor he kept producing a
bare minimum to keep alive and cared little about the
fate of the citydweller or the triumph of world revolution.

— 2 —

THE NEW ECONOMIC POLICY (NEP), 1921-1928

Looming Compromise with Capitalism. By the end of the Civil War the Soviet government came face to face with the possibility of being defeated by economic instead of military challenge. In view of this situation Lenin decided to make a compromise with capitalism. This ideological retreat came to be known as the New Economic Policy or NEP. The retreat was not an easy decision to make; the left wing of the party was by no means convinced that it would solve the problems faced in 1921. But Lenin had no taste for rhetorical contests with his "dreaming opponents." Speaking before the Party Congress Lenin said: "If certain communists were inclined to think it possible in three years to transform the whole economic foundation, to change the very roots of agriculture, they were certainly dreamers; and we must confess to having a few such dreamers among us."

Lenin admitted that in the existing circumstances communism was out of the question and the best the party could expect would be to accept some kind of an ideological mixture of communism and capitalism. The world revolution, he further stated, which the party expected to materialize during the last four years, failed to arrive on schedule. Meanwhile one had to cope with realities without betraying one's idealism. Marking the fourth anniversary of the revolution Lenin bluntly admitted that the party was carried away by a "wave of exaltation" and "military enthusiasm" in the application of communism. (*See Reading No. 9.*) Facts of the revolution taught the government differently, and reality compelled the party

21

leaders to turn to a new strategy—the New Economic Policy.

The New Economic Policy was officially adopted by the Tenth Congress of the Communist Party in March 1921. The policy went into effect at the time when the Red Army was engaged in crushing the Kronstadt mutiny. As it was adopted the policy was not precisely defined, and as it was carried out it demanded much clarification. In principle it could be regarded as a compromise based on trial and error; it was an effort to combine private and socialist doctrines in order to extricate the nation from a desperate situation. The new policy granted official recognition and economic status to the middle class and to the ambitious peasantry formerly frowned upon.

To some communists this was nothing less than sheer betrayal of socialism to capitalism. If concessions had to be made, some party doctrinaires argued, it would have to be worked out between peasants and workers, but there can be no yielding to capitalism. On the other hand the champions of the opposite view contended that NEP would afford the government the eagerly sought and badly needed respite. The policy was bound, they argued, to win the cooperation of the peasantry. The supporters of Lenin admitted the unethical ideological character of NEP, but justified it on grounds that it constituted a temporary tactical retreat to afford greater gain at a more opportune moment. It was not a betrayal of principles but a deviation strategy: instead of a swift offensive it became a slow siege. Meanwhile, to employ Lenin's metaphor, the party had to hold on firmly to the "dominating heights of the economy" for future action. How successful this strategy would be Lenin himself was not too certain. To quote his own observation:

> The fundamental question, from the point of strategy, is, Who will take sooner advantage of this new situation? Who will win? The capitalist whom we are now letting in through the door or even through several doors which we ourselves ignore and which will open independently of us and against us? Or the sovereign power of the proletariat?

Another debate took place at the Tenth Congress of the Communist Party along with the subject of the implications of the NEP. The subject was the place of the trade unions in the Soviet state. Whereas Trotsky and his followers favored the "militarization of the working class" by forming a labor army in which the trade unions would act as some sort of brigade, while trade union officers would act as appointees of the state. The critics of this scheme—called the Worker's Opposition—urged instead that factory management be entrusted to the trade unions, who would form a Council of Producers. The trade unions were to guard their class interests, for though the proletariat held political power its members were still liable to carry demoralizing tendencies aggravated by an entrenched bureaucracy. A compromise was finally reached whereby strikes were permissible, but in reality were banned, because the Communist Party soon assumed complete mastery over the trade unions.

Thus NEP became a reality not of free choice but by an urgent need for economic recovery. Had there been a better choice the party would have gladly accepted a more palatable course; having no alternative Soviet leaders, consoled by the fact that they still held "the strategic heights," cast their ideological pride aside and compromised in order to gain time and master the craft of statesmanship. Once the economic situation had improved and the state had recovered from its recent war shocks, the chasm between countryside and city would be bridged and then the party would return once more to socialism. Meanwhile, if capitalism was permitted to reenter Soviet society, at least it was leashed by a proletarian party that held supreme political power.

Agriculture under NEP. One of the cardinal aims of NEP was to win the mass of the peasantry to the side of the Soviet government and restore normal exchange of products between town and country. To this end a number of radical measures were undertaken. One of the measures was a food tax which simultaneously abolished the requisitions of surplus grain practiced during the recent years of War Communism. The peasant was now able to pay taxes either in cash or in kind, while after 1923 he was to pay in money only. "From now on," an official explanation read, "requisitioning is abolished and a tax in kind on agricultural products is introduced instead. Every peasant must now realize and bear in mind that the more land he cultivates, the greater will be his surplus of grain which remains his personal property." The surplus produce the peasant was entitled to dispose of in a free competitive market.

The amount of tax was determined by the amount of surplus produce the peasant possessed for disposal in the free market. And the surplus was determined by the net produce above the minimum per capita subsistence. The incentive would be to increase the surplus volume in order to derive a maximum profit. By doing this, however, the Soviet government had inadvertently introduced a number of significant changes. One of these was the implied admission of free trade; another was recognizing, though with some circumspect and complex rules, the profit motive. A further implication was that a free market, once recognized, called for a stabilized currency. It should also be added that the state presumably had to acknowledge its failure and discontinue its former system of centralized distribution of foodstuffs and other commodities. Agriculture, as well as industry, was gradually passing to a regular system of money transaction on a commercial basis.

The state still claimed to be the sole owner of all land. The only claim the peasant could have was as long as he tilled the land. But he was unable either to lease, to sell, or to bequeath it. Ambitious peasants might be able to rent extra land; they could hire needed labor, own domestic animals, and buy or rent necessary mechanical equipment. On this point, however, much debate was held and sharp differences remained among the party members throughout the NEP years. Opponents asserted and with a degree of plausibility that such a policy must invariably result in the entrenchment of the kulak, the prosperous tight-fisted anti-Soviet peasant element. Once this peasant minority reasserted itself, they argued, it would be most difficult to dislodge it. In the end it would invariably bear serious political consequences.

Industry under NEP. Appropriate changes also followed in industry. One of the most striking was industrial decentralization and the formation of units known as *trusts.* Approximately 9 percent of industrial enterprises were regarded as vital to the national economy and therefore had remained under exclusive state control. Heavy industries were retained under the centralized state administration though they were managed now on a commercial basis. Others were given administrative and financial independence or the government was willing to lease to foreign concessionaires. Small enterprises could be taken over by cooperatives or private businessmen. Some medium-sized plants were taken over jointly by state and private management. Regardless under what management industrial units were operated, they all based their policies on profit motives. A tighter labor discipline was urged throughout, and labor earnings were to be figured on the principle of "each according to his ability."

Managers of industrial enterprises that were not included in the state-operated units quickly seized the initiative with the hope of expanding profit-making operations. But they discovered that much of their envisioned prospects were in conflict with reality. Some therefore soon sought to join other similar or related units and form trusts of their own. Others discovered formidable difficulties in procurement of necessary raw materials or products except through government contracts or other forms of government assistance. It was soon found that the free initiative counted upon was often hampered by various rules, regulations, and contractual provisions. Although the precise status of the trusts were defined by a decree of April 1923, they differed in organization, commercial independence, or financial capacity. During the twenties the trusts had undergone many changes caused largely either by internal changes or compelled by experience such as financial difficulties or external developments and government rulings.

The New Currency. Since NEP implied a money economy, it became necessary to stabilize the currency as well as establish a banking and credit system that would be recognized within as well as without the country. Toward this the State Bank was reopened in November 1921. At the same time the government publicly announced its intention to restore trade, industry, and agriculture, and it pledged to establish a "sound monetary circulation." Eventually the old worthless paper currency was withdrawn while a new one came to take its place. In 1923 the State Bank also issue a newly stabilized currency, the *chervonets*. A year later the depreciated ruble was withdrawn entirely and the chervonets took its place. Twenty-five percent of the chervonets (1 chervonets was equivalent to 10 rubles) was backed by foreign currency and gold, while 70 percent was guaranteed by short-term negotiable notes. By 1923 the State Bank and its 116 affiliated offices were functioning throughout the Soviet Union. A year later about 2,500 savings banks were opened, adding further stability to the financial state of affairs.

Domestic and Foreign Trade. The system of distribution as practiced during the period of War Communism was now discarded. Many items formerly distributed by the state the consumer now had to obtain on the free market. Along with free-trade enterprises the Soviet government also recognized corporate trade organizations, or cooperatives. These were independent of any state organizations and acted as free enterprises. They enrolled members of their own choice and allocated membership fees as they saw fit. The government anticipated that the cooperatives would act as an effective check on private trade and protect the consumer from exorbitant prices charged by private businessmen. By the end of 1928 the total trade turnover of the cooperatives exceeded the amount of private trade by almost three to one.

On one point, foreign trade, the Soviet government remained unyielding regardless of all criticism presented during the Twelfth Congress of the Communist Party. The prevailing view was that foreign trade must remain a state monopoly regardless of all other concessions. Foreign trade was considered too vital a weapon to be passed into the hands of ideological foes. No tariff walls, it was believed, could withstand foreign interference with industrial planning or preclude inundation of the home market with imported commodities. The economic structure of Soviet Russia was too weak to face competition with advanced industrial nations.

That the government was well aware of the ideological dangers which NEP presented was evidenced by the control the state had constantly endeavored to exercise over free enterprise. It is precisely this situation which resulted in the state of confusion that often prevailed during the NEP period. Side by side with the quasi-free economy there coexisted a quasi-socialist economy in a society headed by an omnipotent Communist Party. The men in power endeavored to hold the reins of control, though with only various degrees of success. It is where control was less successful that the party became concerned. Not long before his death Lenin had realized and had to admit that private enterprise proved stronger than the party. He urged his comrades to learn how to trade with the capitalist world lest it would fall completely into the hands of the Nepmen. The harder the lessons were driven home the firmer the Soviet government held on to the exclusive right of the state to foreign trade.

The Approaching End. The constant suspicion with which the Communist Party had been watching the NEP as an ideologically inimical force gradually compelled the government to reassess the entire situation. This was further necessitated by the general international situation, the depression of 1929, the ascendancy of Nazism to power, and the Japanese aggression in China. Critics of the NEP pointed out that despite the lack of support from abroad and the noncooperative peasantry at home, Soviet Russia must initiate a more carefully planned industrialization program on a scale free enterprise could hardly handle.

An industrial program of such gigantic dimensions as conceived in the late twenties called for an imposition of heavy burdens upon all, and above all upon the peasantry. The Soviet government had to recognize the sad fact that the needed capital for industrialization had to be derived mostly from the rural sections of the country. The prospect of peasant support to be given to the urban portion of the nation for economic rewards to be received in the distant future was by no means a bright one. Reasonable as the arguments seemed to the government, the peasantry wished no part in or of the program. Yet many communists insisted on initiating the program of "socialist planning" as speedily as possible. The longer the delay, these argued, the more difficult the task was bound to be, and it was felt that lack of such a program would eventually threaten the very existence of the Soviet regime.

In the field of industry the government seemed to feel on secure grounds with its program. The state had initially retained complete control over a good deal of industrial production; it was now only a matter of intensified tempo and expansion. Toward this end the State Planning Commission, or *Gosplan*, began to prepare all appropriate steps toward a set goal—national self-sufficiency, or at least a maximum of economic independence. The economic dependence of the Soviet state upon the outside, unfriendly world was sufficient stimulus for decisive action toward a greater degree of economic freedom from reliance upon the West.

There was less assurance in the realm of agriculture, where desperate efforts were made to keep the peasantry in line. The fear that small individual landholdings might assume too great a power continued throughout the twenties. It was this fear that prompted the Land Code of 1922, which intended to remind the peasantry once again specifically that the land remained the property of the state, although the tillers of the soil were privileged to exploit it freely. The law definitely forbade all private land transactions in the form of purchase, sale, mortage, gift, or bequest. Another measure resisting the potent individualistic sense of land ownership of the peasantry was the official encouragement of agricultural cooperatives, which under the NEP came in as a substitute for the more rigidly enforced commune during the period of War Communism. Within five years nearly six million peasants joined the various cooperative organizations. It was the hope of the government that the agricultural cooperatives would aid the poorer peasants and prevent the rise of a kulak class—the bitterest enemy of socialism.

And yet "bourgeois" economy continued to be a disturbing factor. There was a deep and justified suspicion that the NEP did not carry forward a socialist economy; admittedly, though, it did aid considerably in restoring and stabilizing the shaken foundation of the national economy. Communists readily acknowledged that the net result of the NEP experience was of appreciable advantage. (*See Reading No. 10.*) But, aside from the speedier progress required by national and international conditions, critics also pointed to the fact that the economic benefits of the NEP carried with them the peril of ideological annihilation. The government soon came to realize that it was facing the alternative of either drifting with the quasicapitalistic NEP and thereby betraying its political faith or adhering to its ideological principles and reverting to a socialist economy.

Animated debates during the middle twenties revolved around two issues: the delay of the so ardently hoped-for world revolution and the problem of the NEP. The daring experiment in "strategic retreat" and the holding of the "commanding heights" left more problems than it answered. It carried within itself many theoretical contradictions which became sharper as years advanced. The Bolshevik revolution started with "total" communism and ended with concessions to capitalists; it started with collectivism and wound up with tolerating kulak elements. Battling capitalism with one hand, with the other the government beckoned foreign capitalists to assist in the building of the Soviet Union, the citadel of world revolution. Originally combating free trade, the NEP now established free retail markets. Small wonder that these contradictions kept bewildering many communists and weakened unanimity of purpose within the party. It kept undermining faith abroad in Soviet policies, for there was no certainty as to when "transitional policies" would revert to "pure socialism." It must have been an excruciating experience for a party like the communists, as Sir Bernard Pares had keenly observed, "to hold the power on condition that you let the greater part of the population do the opposite to what you wished." It was a most extraordinary situation: the more consistently one adhered to the doctrines of the Communist Party, the greater was his heresy as far as the government was concerned.

Contribution of NEP. Putting ideological aspects aside, it is necessary to recognize some of the contributions NEP made toward the restoration of economic stability between 1921 and 1928, even though the stability did not move along a path visualized by communist theoreticians. Despite all restrictions and handicaps caused by the ever-vigilant, suspicious, and interfering apparatus of the state, agriculture and industry made impressive strides. The figures cited in Part II (*See Reading No. 10.*) illustrate the progress attained in the production of some vital materials by 1928 compared with the prewar year 1913.

During the NEP period employment increased, wages improved, and many workers who had left the cities during the civil war and famine began to return to their former vocations. Still there were cries for skilled labor in many industries, an appalling need for the replacement of worn out or outdated machinery, and a shortage of capital for technological improvement. Business began to recover from the jolts of War Communism and trade was stimulated, even under restricted freedom; a balanced budget was attained within a few years and a degree of prosperity was achieved within a relatively short period. The recuperative power of the nation was a marvel to many people at home and abroad. But it was this rapid comeback that disheartened and alarmed the orthodox Marxists who feared the ascendancy of a social order which they had too recently torn down at such cost. A Nepman's triumph might produce an impression upon the nation and the world that the revolution was wrong —a frightfully wasted effort.

Whither Now? The NEP was unquestionably an economic and ideological retreat, but how far was that retreat to be carried on? When and where was the line to be drawn? Many communists lived under a sincere apprehension that the party was facing ideological self-destruction and that the entire faith became meaningless unless the retreat were halted and the "socialist offensive" resumed. Many pointed out the social demoralization that had evolved from the new policy: a new bourgeois had risen, the Nepman, the *nouveaux riche* who threatened to wipe out all revolutionary gains. What was even more frightening to these alarmists was the possibility that the NEP air might demoralize the party itself. The increased propensity toward profit motives, toward living amid still prevailing poverty, the craving for light petit bourgeois entertainment—all this offended some and aroused jealousy among others. Temptation was great to join the profiteers and quickly get rich. Purges of party members whose NEP flesh began to overcome their Marxian spirit became a frequent phenomenon. A loud cry arose demanding action against the poison that threatened the entire social body. Many asked themselves: Was it worthwhile to have shed all the blood and wreck the entire economy of a nation in order to build a heaven for the Nepman in the city and for the kulak in the countryside?

Even more distressing to Marxist thinkers was the situation in the villages. To win the peasants' cooperation the Soviet government was forced to make continuous concessions at the expense of communist ideology. Realizing the importance of gaining stability and economic improvement, the government continued to appease the peasantry by granting it greater freedom from state control. After the first concessions that the Soviet government made in March 1921, there followed others which clearly indicated that the officials feared any conflict with the peasants. It was believed that until political and economic consolidation had been attained, any antagonistic agrarian policy was playing with fire. The peasant sensed this fear and with each concession became bolder in his insistence upon further reforms to his liking. But his vision was narrow, his taste petit bourgeois, and he had no care for the needs of the city and the complex industrial problems.

During the middle of the 1920's the government reluctantly followed a moderate policy by tolerating an "enrich yourself" atmosphere. The individual peasant was granted the right to hire labor and to rent more land. This provoked much opposition within the party ranks, but opponents were labeled Trotskyites and effectively silenced for the time being. Occasionally critics would voice disapproval of pampering the kulak element, as was done by Kamenev or Zinoviev, sharply condemning the advocate of peasant appeasement, Bukharin. It may be of interest to note that Stalin at first followed a middle-of-the-road policy. It was only after he silenced both sides of the opposition that he determined to adopt measures that shocked both the left and the right opponents. The bitter struggle was not so much caused by personality clashes, individual ambitions, or dogmatic tenacity as by a more practical and urgent question. It revolved around the bewildering issue of how to extract most effectively agricultural surplus production as capital so urgently needed for industrialization.

Criticism of the situation came from both the rightists and leftists of the party. If the former hoped that agricultural progress could be assured by enterprising kulaks, the latter regarded the system a reversal to the days of Stolypin. In the end, they predicted, it would result in small strip farming and retard true progress; the only way in which the problem might be met would be by collectivization and mechanization of agriculture.

We have seen how this fear on behalf of the government led to concessions: the peasant was allowed to sell his produce on a free market instead of surrendering it to the government, which limited his obligations to specified tax payments. He was permitted to hire workers and lease land for a term as long as twelve years. In 1923 a law was promulgated legalizing individual farming. The peasant received all these concessions, admired them, asked for more, and continued to oppose the government by passive yet quite effective means. He always managed to evade his tax payments or turn over less grain than the law had prescribed, thereby accumulating arrears, and then claiming reductions. Within five years the arrears came to amount to some 45 percent. This shortage seriously handicapped the government in its desperate effort to export grain in exchange for badly needed foreign machinery. Sabotage on the part of the peasant continued, and it proved a deadly instrument.

Increased speculation on the grain market exasperated the authorities. The richer peasants not only refused to yield their grain to the government, but bought out the grain in the fall when prices were low and then resold it in the spring when prices had been raised. The cost of food in the cities soared. The government was help-less each year to stem the vicious though understandable practice.

There were other forebodings of equally serious nature. One was the difficulty of extracting surpluses from a countryside where the economy was based on small peasant households. In a modern economy such agricul-ture is doomed to inefficiency and obsolete technical methods. Small landholding could keep the peasant alive, but hardly shoulder a modern dynamic economy. There would be adequate production for the local but not na-tional market, not to mention production for export markets. To attain the latter required large-scale pro-duction with the aid of modern science and the latest technological equipment. In a Soviet state this meant only one thing—socialized agriculture, enabling the gov-ernment to obtain adequate marketable surpluses.

— 3 —

THE FIRST
FIVE YEAR PLAN,
1928-1933

Planned Economy Enters the Stage. Between 1921 and 1928 economic policies were frequently discussed and at times heatedly debated, and, surprisingly, in an atmosphere of considerable tolerance. There were those who insisted that priority be given to agriculture, and there were those who maintained that industry should enjoy all preference. Among the latter were differences of opinion as to the tempo of industrialization, some arguing in favor of rapid speed and others advising a slower pace. But whatever these opinions were, it may be noted that Soviet economics displayed unusual dynamism at a time when the West witnessed a high degree of post-war fatigue. It was only with the termination of the NEP that the enthusiasm was dampened. The high-centralization management, the brutal enforcement of the planned economy, the more shocking enforcement of collectivization, all combined to reveal some harsh aspects of the newly adopted policy. Many economists refused to agree with Stalin and paid dearly for their views. A smaller number accepted the general line of policy and dourly consented to work in one capacity or another in the enforcement of the planned economy. Thus began the shift from the NEP to the five year plans, marking truly an economic revolution.

The Economic Revolution. The year 1928 marks a milestone on the long road toward realization of the aims of the Russian Revolution. The stupendous program set for the government by the Fifteenth Congress of the Communist Party in December 1927 indicated a complete victory of the Stalin faction over the Trotsky opposition group and of "socialism in a single country" over international socialism. The opponents of Stalin—Trotsky, Zinoviev, Kamenev, and others—were banished. At the same time the congress opened a "socialist offensive" along the front of the entire national economy.

The duties of elaborating the plan for economic reconstruction were assigned to a commission that had been functioning since 1921, the State Planning Commission, or *Gosplan*. By the beginning of 1928 the Commission produced what came to be known as the First Five Year Plan, which officially went into effect on October 1, 1928. The plan envisioned the complete industrial and agrarian reorganization of the sprawling Soviet Union. It aimed at a relocation of industrial centers to correspond to the areas of natural resources—a step which would not only eliminate costly long hauls but remove industry from possible war zones.

There were many reasons for this Herculean revolutionary undertaking. Apart from a desire to prevent the complete defeat of the revolution by the forces of the NEP, there were other, more weighty reasons for this reversal of the retreat tactics begun in 1921. Beneath official declarations there ran a deep desire to break loose from Western capitalism. The Soviet government was in desperate need of long-term credits, which the capitalist nations refused until some satisfactory solution of prerevolutionary debts should be secured. Short-term credits were both embarrassing and costly. It was abundantly clear that Moscow could not continue soliciting for loans, humbly inviting benevolent foreign concessionaries to develop the country and lagging behind the rest of Europe in the race to restore crippled economies and armed strength. The political sky was full of war signs; relations between the Soviet Union and European nations were at best frigidly correct, at worst openly hostile. As the Soviet government faced the situation at home and abroad, it became increasingly clear that it had to alter the social order in a manner wherein the dictatorship of the proletariat would be assured the vital role; it had to prevent the hostile peasantry and petit bourgeoisie, the Nepman, from entrenching themselves to a degree where it would become impossible to dislodge them from economic and political influence.

The Communist Party could not fail to observe that whereas the NEP had aided in raising the agricultural output to the pre-1914 level (*see Reading No. 10*), the marketable surplus for the cities and for export was only 30 percent of its prewar volume. Constantly haunted by fear of foreign attack, the government felt compelled to shake off dependence on foreign supplies. And because the nation's strength depended on modern industry as well as on mechanized, scientific agriculture, neither imports of industrial commodities nor of agricultural produce would suffice. This the men who drew the Five Year Plan blueprints had to take into account, and they thus prepared for a vast industrial, agricultural, and psychological revolution of a scope and speed that hardly found any historical precedent.

The Planning. As mentioned above, the organization in charge of the overall economy plan was concentrated in the State Planning Commission. This commission was assisted by numerous state agencies such as those that were in charge of labor discipline and of trade unions. The basis of economic planning entirely disregarded old principles such as free market play of supply and demand.

The plan was based not on considerations of market demand, but on what the national plan called for. Nor was what was more profitable considered, but what was more vital within the entire pattern of the state economy. If the plan demanded an emphasis upon a designated amount of steel, iron, coal, or kilowatt-hours of electricity, regardless of loss or profit, this enjoyed the priority in production. If certain commodities were assigned priority production, regardless of cost, the State Bank would grant the necessary loans. Here is perhaps one of the most striking departures of the planned socialist economy from the capitalist system. Some of the other features to be noted were the absence of interest on loans, allocated capital investments, or complete disregard of cost interest on capital amortization charges, or depreciation.

The First Five Year Plan in Action. The blueprint of the First Five Year Plan fills nearly a thousand close pages of statistical data. It aimed at centralization and industrialization by means of rational production and distribution. The extraordinary features of the plan were the socialist *method,* the speed, the faith in its fulfillment, and the precision with which the entire project was to be carried out. The undertaking came to release a national momentum bound to carry profound effects upon the country. The plan contemplated an investment of 64 billion rubles, half of which was to be devoted to industry. Much of the designated sum was to be spent on electrical-chemical-metallurgical combines, electrification and expansion of industries, increase in coal and oil production, and the establishment of a vast chemical industry. In the field of agriculture the plan provided for the expansion of food production. This was to be accomplished by an organization of state and collective farms financed by the state and local administrations. It was calculated that by the end of the First Five Year Plan at least 39 percent of all grain would be provided by collective farms. To avoid exhaustion of the soil under such intensive cultivation, the plan provided for the production of 7 million tons of mineral fertilizers annually.

It would be futile to demonstrate the revolutionary aspects of this gigantic effort by statistical data alone.

These would tell only a small part of the story. Nor would such data be helpful in estimating either the quantitative or qualitative accomplishments during the First Five Year Plan. There was much pride in achievement and as much distress over failures. The serious shortage of skilled labor and trained managerial personnel resulted in many costly blunders. Production cost often proved disproportionately high, while waste of materials or breakage of delicate machinery was quite common.

Even more intangible are the estimates in terms of human toil and deprivation. The sacrifices the Russian people made for the initial progress were staggering. Unable to obtain capital from abroad, it had to be found at home. This meant one thing: the needed capital had to be gotten at the expense of the consumer by curtailing production of essential daily use. By the end of the First Five Year Plan a third of the nation's income was diverted to capital saving. To make it even worse, in order to make the needed purchases abroad the government was compelled to increase exports and thereby reduce the consumer to a bare subsistence. In the end it resulted in untold hardships and privations for which the government could promise only one thing—hope for a better future.

Immediate Effects of the Economic Revolution. The concentrated effort to industrialize and collectivize the economy of the Soviet Union had a profound effect upon national policies. There was less emphasis upon internationalism, which was best demonstrated by the diminishing role of the Third International and the adopted policy of "Socialism in One Country." The demands of the planned economy bred a sense of national pride in achieving a mammoth goal in building a socialist society at a time when all odds were against it and at a time when the rest of the world was in the midst of an unprecedented depression. It contributed to the rise of a national spirit and cultivated a self-assertive belief in "do it alone" in a hostile world that refuses to cooperate in the building of a new economic order.

Investment Capital. The Five Year Plan called for gigantic investment capital. Unable to obtain loans abroad the government employed every conceivable device to

locate capital at home. Production and consumption for
home use was subordinated to the needs of the planning
projects rather than the consumers' demands. Wages and
prices on all industrial and farm produce were artificially
manipulated for the same purpose. The government
wrenched farm produce at set prices and sold it in cities
and towns at another, often deriving profit from such
deals, using the profit for industrial expansion.

Along with the extraordinary sacrifices the Soviet citizen had to make, he also enjoyed a few benefits. Among
these were free public health service, low rent, and inexpensive transportation. But both industrial workers and
peasants paid dearly for these in less measurable though
important ways. The average worker was deprived of a
maximum of consumer articles as a means of carrying
out the state plans of industrialization. The peasant had
to yield every saved ounce of his produce to keep alive
the urban worker. Wherever forced labor could be used
the government utilized it on canal construction, dams,
and other state undertakings in distant corners of the
Soviet Union. Piece work and other devices were applied to add incentive to production.

Labor Legislation. The recently introduced planned
economy demanded a labor discipline which the Stalin
regime applied with particular harshness. Workers noted
for absenteeism, for shifting jobs, or for slovenliness were
liable to most severe disciplinary action. This could include banishment to forced labor camps or imprisonment.
Labor unions were utilized by the government in carrying
out the economic program. Ever since the early twenties
the trade unions had lost their independence, to the re-
gret of some old guard party members. Labor lost the
right to strike; and with powerless unions unable to back
the workers or to challenge effectively the enforced discipline, the administration acted without fear during these
crucial years. As the Five Year Plan went into effect the
unions had little to say concerning living conditions,
wages, hours, vacations, or anything else. The government alone determined what was good for society and
the share labor had to contribute to the welfare of the
nation.

Industry. As soon as Stalin began to feel more secure he applied the same policy his opponents had urged upon him during the middle twenties, hoping to free the city from the exasperating dependence upon the peasant. He also hoped to free the U.S.S.R. from economic dependence upon the West, since industrialization was identified with national security. To accomplish these goals no sacrifice was too great and no cost too high; to this end every feasible device was used, every skilled worker was sought and put to work, every branch of science brought into service. Foreign technicians were invited to the Soviet Union to render their aid and native talent sent abroad to gain needed experience. Plans were designed to exploit all resources to be found throughout the Soviet Union. Every able-bodied person was called to duty, and all available capital investment utilized for industrial expansion. Of all the different projects heavy industry stood highest on the priority list, including the production of steel, coal, oil, machinery, electricity, and all means of defense. The consumer was given little concern and left to his devices to manage as best he could. Long-range goals in the field of industrialization were of immediate concern which stripped the average citizen of most vital daily necessities. Basic indicators of the economic development as projected under the first five year plan and gross production of census industries during the same period are cited elsewhere. (*See Readings Nos. 11 and 12.*)

Agriculture. At the initiation of the First Five Year Plan the Soviet Union was still basically an agrarian state: the major portion of the nation was engaged in agriculture, and most of the rural population consisted of an estimated 25 million independent peasant households. It is along this front that a bitter test was soon to be renewed between the state and the peasant when the former had decided upon the enforcement of the economic program. The basic issue was the conversion of the individual household farms into larger units, into a collective system. Huge state farms were set up where local conditions favored their establishment. The two, the collective and the state farm units, were part of a single state project—the establishment of a national socialized agrarian economy directed by a centralized state administration.

During the summer of 1928 the Soviet government had still hoped to leave the individual small and middle-sized farms undisturbed; it would only insist upon faithful fulfillment of the assessed grain and foodstuffs tax. The old agricultural economy would therefore be left without serious disturbance. This proved false and in the spring of 1929 Stalin ordered rigorous measures against the peasants who refused to cooperate and pay the tax. And even at this stage individual peasant holdings were not yet altered. But the entire program was now at stake and the chance of conflict seemed greater if the program of industrialization was to be carried out successfully.

Collectivization Violently Enforced. Undertaking collectivization amounted to a socioeconomic revolution in every sense. Collectivization's immediate goal, the elimination of the kulak class, its most determined rural opponent, was in itself a decisive step. It led to a frightful effort to obtain the needed supplies to feed the cities engaged in an equally revolutionary industrial effort. The government was determined to force the peasantry into this gigantic reconstruction program and to crush any resistance at whatever cost.

Violence was soon provoked by the compulsory assessments for the purchases of loans, by the penalities invoked for refusal to yield the grain tax, and by the confiscation of hidden stocks. Violent clashes between peasants and army units sent to collect grain became frequent. When the peasants realized that they would be defeated in open battle they resorted to their old tactics of evasion by curtailing production. This only intensified further the struggle, and the government became convinced that only a complete collectivization program would be the solution. The challenge was undertaken with serious misgivings, but once the decision was made the government did not falter.

The violent struggle with the kulaks began as a punitive operation. The government did not anticipate the strong resistance it was to encounter. The mistake the government made was in anticipating resistance only from the minority kulak elements, while hoping that the majority of the peasants would support the government. To its great disappointment it learned that there was hardly a peasant—kulak or otherwise—who was willing to deliver grain assessments or who was enthusiastic about abandoning the personal land-holding system. The battle soon assumed the character of a conflict between the government and the peasantry. The forces were uneven in strength, and by the spring of 1930 the peasant had to admit his defeat. Centuries of cumulated traditions and deeply entrenched habits had to yield to more recent mechanized methods in agriculture accompanied by an alien system of collectivism. This was more than a revolution: it began to assume the nature of a social cataclysm. For a short while the government risked its very existence when it decided to destroy traditional agrarianism and start a new economic order in which it had more faith than experience. The country was again literally on the brink of a civil war.

Since the destruction of the old economy was going on at a faster pace than the organization of the collective system, there was a catastrophic dislocation in agriculture. The transition period brought the nation face to face with a crisis that literally threatened the entire existence of the Soviet regime. Pressure was put on with crushing weight and the reorganization was at such a tempo that millions of peasants paid with their freedom or their lives for their resistance. But the backbone of the peasant resistance was crushed, though at a shocking price and risk. Henceforth collectivization became the pattern in the agricultural economy of the Soviet Union. It was a gamble driven with relentless and brutal force.

It was unfortunate that amid the formidable difficulties the nation had already come to face in the urban communities due to the industrialization program was added the violent enforcement of collectivization in the countryside. That mechanized agriculture was desirable but could not be applied as long as small strip farming prevailed was clear. It was equally understandable that industrialization was essential, even though without the benefits of foreign capital; that the industrial program had to be assured of regular delivery of foodstuffs did not require extra proof. Whether the government succeeded in convincing the peasantry to contribute its share to the economic transformation of the country remains doubtful. Only time will prove which side was historically right. Even the party itself was by no means unanimous in its decision to pursue the harsh Stalin line. There were many members who questioned the wisdom of forced collectivization and regarded the policy untimely, bound to fail. There were opponents who, though accepting the changes in principle, were less certain about the pace and urged caution in antagonizing the countryside. Prominent right-wing party members, such as Kalinin, Tomsky, Rykov, and Bukharin, opposed the dangerous gamble. But Stalin insisted on going ahead with the "squeezing out" of the kulak as the enemy of the socialist system. (*See Reading Nos. 13-15, 17.*)

The Collective Farms. Officially the collectivization program was begun in January 1930. Some 100,000 collective farms (Kolkhoz), with an area of about 16 million hectares,* were planned by the government. In accordance with the revised statute of 1935, adopted by the All-Union Congress, the collective farm was recognized as a permanent institution. It was regulated by the following provisions: When a collective was formed the members were given a charter which formulated the legal land tenure and governed the relationship between the collective farm and the state, as well as the life and work within that farm. Land was given to the collective as the property of the state and the people tilling it. This land was conferred on the collective for permanent usufruct and could not be deeded, leased, bought, or sold by the members. The allotted land might be expanded, but in no circumstances reduced, in area.

Parts of the designated area were assigned for personal use, as in vegetable gardens; this personal allotment might vary in size, but it could not exceed one hectare. Every member of a collective was also entitled to own livestock for personal use and buildings for housing, which were not subject to collectivization. Each member had a right to claim a share in the profit of the collective in pro-

* One hectare equals 2.4 acres.

portion to his invested effort. Before dividends were paid out, however, the collective farm had to first dispose of its common obligations: a certain amount of produce must be sold to the state at a set price, and a designated amount must go as payment for machine service and maintenance. The balance might be disposed of in the open market. Expulsion of a collective farmer could take place only by a decision of the general meeting of the collective at which two thirds of all the members were in attendance. The expelled member was entitled to appeal to higher authorities, demanding a revision of the decision, if he chose.

The collective farms varied in size, some of them incorporating as many as four or five thousand landholders. The right of individual farmers to rent land and hire labor was suspended; the land of the kulaks might be confiscated and the former owners banished from the rural communities. On the other hand, the peasants who joined the collective farms were equipped with modern agricultural machinery and allowed many privileges not given individual householders. Peasants could still claim some small garden plots, but the basis of the agricultural economy was now the rigorously enforced system of collectivism. New stringent regulations were adopted which limited the time the peasant could devote to his garden plots, allowing him more days per week to spend in the collective field. Authorities in charge of either the collective or the state farms also had the power of labor discipline. To stimulate production all sorts of devices were employed—public praise, awards of medals, titles such as labor hero, special bonuses, vacations, trips to the capital and elsewhere. On the other hand, any lack of enthusiasm was bound to cause suspicion of sabotage—a dreadful offense punishable by lifetime imprisonment or even death.

Only the state was to determine what was good for the farmer. When the state decided on any given priorities the peasant's sentiments were brushed aside. The peasant did not take this benevolent despotism in any spirit of humility. As the government began to enact collectivization peasants in many parts of the country violently rebelled against it. So serious was the violence to become that the government was forced to retreat and acknowledge that it erred in its tempo of enforcement because of "dizziness from success." The government therefore decided to retreat temporarily and returned the right of the peasant to claim his small private plot. This constituted a partial though by no means a decisive victory. Collectivization simply progressed at a lesser pace: an estimated quarter of a million collective farms were eventually established to sustain the country at large.

Of the various devices the government employed in maintaining control over the collective farms, one of the more effective was the Machine Tractor Station (MTS). The MTS controlled all the government-owned mechanized equipment—tractors, combines, threshers—without which plowing, seeding, and harvesting would not be possible. Each station serviced between 60 and as high as 300 collective farms, depending on the size of each farm. For the use of this machinery the government exacted a share of the harvested crops. The men who operated the MTS were government employees who not only operated the machines but supervised the collective farms.

The initial steps in collectivization were filled with difficulties. The mechanized equipment was lacking or inadequate, while the machinery that was available was operated by inexperienced labor and often suffered from abuse and the inability to find needed parts. In many cases the recalcitrant peasant remained unimpressed by all the favors the government lavished upon him and continued to cherish hope of a return to his former plot or privately owned land. Many of the peasants, as a protest and in order to escape the dreaded classification as kulaks, systematically kept reducing production, slaughtered their livestock, and rid themselves of their movable property. The wholesale destruction of cattle and the surrender of only underfed and worthless stock to the collective farms became truly alarming. In round figures, this is what happened to the livestock population between 1929 and 1933 (*see table opposite*):

Such mass slaughter the government regarded as deliberate sabotage and took appropriate measures. Special local committees, Kombeds or Committees of Poor Peas-

	1929	1930	1933
	(in millions of head)		
horses	34	30	15
cattle	67	52	38
sheep & goats	147	108	50
hogs	20	13	12

ants, were advised to take over the land and inventories of the kulaks. In many parts of the country spontaneous and arbitrary action by local authorities and individual peasants intensified the internicine struggle and led to serious property damage. In other localities kulaks put the torch to their property rather than submit to collectivization.

The specter of civil war halted even the hand of Stalin. This did not mean that Stalin accepted defeat; he merely interpreted the gravity of the moment as a party success which had gone to its head ("dizziness from success") and promised hereafter a more lenient and cautious policy. It also meant, after the first experience, the government would proceed more methodically. Stalin thought that the trouble developed because the "Leninist principle" had been violated—collective farms must be voluntary and not forced enterprises—and second, collectivization had been applied with complete disregard for diversity of local conditions, and the collective standard had been applied too rigidly. Finally, some party members, made conceited and opinionated by their initial success, exceeded their authority. The result was a serious famine in 1932-1933. Many peasants took advantage of Stalin's "urge but not force" order and began to drift away from the collectives, though with no great success. (*See Reading No. 16.*)

The State Farms. Another kind of farm management was the state farm (*sovkhoz*). The First Five Year Plan figured that by the end of 1930 the state farms would have an area of more than 5 million hectares in full operation. These farms were to operate differently from the collective farms. The latter can be regarded as a cooperative enterprise: by the end of each summer, after discharging its obligations to the government, the collective would divide the gains among its members. The individual share would depend on the annual earnings of the collective farm.

The state farm was an entirely different enterprise. The farm was completely government owned and operated; the workers were state-employed and were paid on a regular monthly basis regardless of the farm's annual income, and were therefore assured of a more stable income. Farm equipment on the state farms was, and is, usually more up to date, better attended to by expert mechanics, and for that reason in better condition.

For none too clear reasons, however, the state farms have never been completely successful. After nearly a quarter of a century of operations the state farms amounted to about 10 percent of the total area under cultivation. In part this is probably explained by the fact that they operate at a deficit covered by government subsidies. This is also partly explained by the low prices the government pays the state farms for the produce. Whatever the reasons for their limited success the opinion among some Soviet leaders has been that they should be discontinued and the inventory turned over to the collective farms. (*On the categories of state farms in 1938 in accordance with the nature of their farming, see Reading Nos. 19-20.*)

— 4 —

THE SECOND FIVE YEAR PLAN, 1933-1938

The Second Five Year Plan Goes into Operation. The Second Five Year Plan went into effect on January 1, 1933. By 1938 80 percent of the national production was the output of the industries constructed between

1928 and 1938. The first plan might be considered as the painful initial step in the direction of national industrialization and the agonizing experiences in the collectivization and mechanization of agriculture. The second plan set out goals that emanated from the first one: consolidation of industrial advances, doubling production in the newly established plants, improvement in quality of production and reduction of cost, and expansion in construction of transportation facilities.

If the First Five Year Plan aimed at complete industrialization of the country, the second plan was accompanied by the lofty aspiration "to eliminate exploitation of man by man." If the first plan laid stress on heavy industry, the second one held out dim promise to devote more attention to production of consumer goods insofar as production of them did not interfere with national defense. Investment capital for light industries was slightly increased, and production of consumer goods was expected to rise proportionately. The new plan hoped to double the production of footwear and foodstuffs and to treble school supplies.

But heavy industry still enjoyed priority, whether in construction of new plants or expansion of production in plants already constructed. The second plan called for new blast furnaces and rolling mills which more than doubled the output of steel and pig iron—there was an urgent demand for the production of nonferrous metals, which were still being obtained from abroad. Particularly stressed were nickel, copper, tin, aluminum, and zinc, in view of the expanded electrical industry. Most of these were to be developed in western and central Siberia and in the Caucasus, and others in the north. During the later war years these industries came to play a vital part in the war effort. In an effort to reduce the dependence upon imports from the West, machine-tool production was to be trebled. In view of the increased war danger not only was general industrial production to be accelerated, but industrial centers were strategically distributed throughout the country to render them less vulnerable to air attacks.

Search for New Resources. The First Five Year Plan had already made it sufficiently clear that the vital coal and iron industries of the south were precariously exposed to military danger. For this reason the government began to urge extensive geological surveys in order to locate possible deposits elsewhere. One of the results was a plan to link the coking-coal deposits of Kuznetsk in Siberia with the ores of the Urals to form a huge combine for iron and steel production. The two centers, 1,250 miles apart, were to be linked by a double-track rail line. The Ural-Kuznetsk combine was destined to become a vital industrial unit and Kuznetsk a coal basin second only to the Donets Basin in the southern Ukraine. Surveys soon discovered coal in other areas, notably in Kazakhstan (Karaganda), southeast of the Urals, which was even more conveniently located to the Ural center.

Surveys were also begun in the Arctic, where potential resources were long presumed. Sizable settlements sprang up in the far north.* The project was accompanied by the construction of a 700-mile railroad running southward to carry the coal. Much of the work was done by forced labor prisoners such as those described by Solzhenitsyn in his celebrated book entitled *One Day in the Life of Ivan Denisovich*. South of Vorkuta, slightly below the Arctic Circle, there developed an oil-producing center at Ukhta.

In 1933 the White and Baltic seas were linked by a canal, dug by convict labor within less than two years. Four years later the 80-mile canal linking the Moscow and Volga rivers was completed. This last required huge hydrotechnical structures with eleven mammoth ferroconcrete locks. Powerful propeller pumps along the 80-mile route force the Volga water into seven huge reservoirs, the largest of which, near Moscow, covers an area of 126 square miles. Today seagoing vessels stop at Khimki on the Moscow River, only a few miles outside the capital, on their way to the Caspian Sea via the Moscow-Volga Canal. By making navigable the fairly shallow Moscow River and linking it with the Volga, a

---

* One of these, unfortunately carries sad memories of the ill-famed forced labor camp at Vorkuta, located approximately 800 miles from Murmansk in the Pechora coal basin, 70 miles north of the Arctic Circle.

vital inland waterway was established that carries annually a large passenger and freight traffic.

Transportation. Prior to 1930 there were few highways beyond the large cities. Water transport was in a sad state and badly lacked river-port facilities. The worn railroad equipment and poor condition of the railbeds impeded traffic speed. As urban population expanded and industrialization kept advancing the need of transportation facilities kept increasing. Not only locally, but nationally the demand for increased transportation facilities kept rising. Delivery of raw materials to industrial centers and the transportation of finished commodities from the cities sharpened the crisis. The strain on the existing system was such that unless quick measures were undertaken a complete collapse in the entire transportation system might become imminent.

Several railroads were constructed during this time which proved strategically as well as economically valuable shortly after their completion. Among these was the line north of Baikal to Komsomolsk, with trunk lines terminating at Khabarovsk and a point on the coast of the Tartar Straits. A branch of the Trans-Siberia Railroad linking Petrozavodsk, Karaganda, and Balkhash was completed in 1930. This road became economically important because it enabled the state to utilize the copper mines of Dzherkazgan and Balkhash. Another line was the Turkestan-Siberian Railway (Turksib) which opened in 1931 and linked the vital centers of Turkestan with the Ural region.

Despite these developments, a serious bottleneck in the national economy was to remain in the field of railway transportation, where growth could not keep pace with the general economic expansion. Whereas passenger traffic in 1937 had increased sixfold and freight fivefold over 1913, track mileage during the same period showed an increase of slightly over 44 percent. It was only in 1940 that the country was able to record a total of 100,000 kilometers (62,140 miles) of track. The increased passenger and freight traffic, with frequently overloaded cars, put a terrific strain on rolling stock, roadbeds, and tracks; simultaneously, standards of upkeep fell. There was considerable inefficiency and frequent disastrous accidents, and the First Five Year Plan, instead of replacing 34,150 kilometers of rails and reconditioning 1,310 kilometers of roadbed, attained only 30 and 59 percent, respectively, of these objectives.

Problems Ahead. The area of poorest achievements was agriculture. Though the battle with the kulaks and the enforcement of the collective system ended successfully, the government, after claiming victory, was left with a tremendous job of consolidation. The bewildered peasants, forced into collective farms, still adhered to the methods of their forefathers; they regarded mechanization of agriculture with characteristic skepticism. It took desperate measures to ease the food shortages in the cities and raise labor productivity. These factors combined to contribute considerably toward the fulfillment of the Second Five Year Plan. Though consumer goods continued to take a second place in general economic planning, even the improvement in this sector had been such as not to be disregarded. The average standard of living, though in Western terms still low, was definitely improved.

The Second Five Year Plan was altered in the course of its fulfillment, largely due to the increased threat of war and the continued rise in armaments. The original plan called for a 150 percent increase in light industry output between 1933 and 1938. By 1936 it was reduced to 100 percent. But in view of the general situation, even the reduced goal was no small achievement, though it fell short of satisfying the long-starved consumer. On the other hand, heavy industry trebled its production in most branches, on the average exceeding the original assignments. The most notable increase was to be found in the newly constructed plants with up-to-date equipment. Thus in the production of railway locomotives and motorized farm equipment the Soviet union became the leading country, and equally impressive gains were made in allied branches of industry. The number of wage and salary earners more than trebled between 1927 and 1938.

By 1938 the average standard of living in the Soviet Union still lagged behind any Western European country, yet the government was still aspiring to outstrip America. An awakened giant was rising, becoming increasingly aware of the potential economic power the land possessed. The determination was not to be content with the successes at the middle of the road. The goal was more than ever to overcome the deep-seated inertia of the peasantry and the low productivity of industrial labor. To gain mastery in technical skills, in modern mass production, in qualitative output as well as quantitative, to improve living standards further though not at the expense of national security, these continued to remain the chief slogans at the time of the adoption of the Third Five Year Plan.

A Reappraisal of Achievements Thus Far. Unable to attract capital from abroad the Soviet government employed all means to utilize whatever meager resources it was able to find. Loans were floated to which at first towns, and only later rural communities, had to subscribe. The bleeding of every ruble of capital brought the nation to a low standard of living, a monotonous, austere daily grind from which the Second Five Year Plan could still hardly relieve the masses. The priorities given at first to industrial building caused a dangerous lag in agriculture, producing a serious food shortage, while the heavy movement of manpower from country to city brought to the urban centers crises reminiscent of the early days of the Industrial Revolution in Western Europe. The food and housing problems in both old and new cities became critical; rapidly diminishing stocks of consumer goods, which had never been plentiful, now hit absolute lows because of the cutting of production. Replenishment of vanishing goods was either impossible or too slow.

To solve the plight of food shortages in urban communities, the government undertook the most hazardous policy of farm collectivization. The policy was met at first with such stubborn resistance and a food blockade by the peasants that the cities were threatened with a virtual famine. In the outburst of violence and hunger a staggering number of peasants perished—how many no one will ever know. Yet even the lowest estimates indicate the frightful price the Russian peasantry with its encrusted habits had to pay for the state-adopted plan of collectivization. In the end the will of the government

proved stronger than the resistance of the peasantry.
Dominated by fear of capitalist encirclement soon to be
accentuated by the ascendancy of Nazism, the Soviet
government refused to relax its program. Resistance in
the countryside was ruthlessly crushed by armed force,
while industrial efficiency was bolstered by special shock
brigades. Whatever one may say in defense of Soviet
policy of the thirties, the grim fact remains that the
initiation of the planned economy accompanied by collectivization constitutes a mournful chapter in modern
history.

The Cost of Planning. Within four years progress
became visible, although the cost was shocking; the
economic character of the Soviet Union had undergone
considerable change. The foundation had been laid for
a profound industrial and agrarian revolution, and the
entire social structure had been modified. A greater co-
herence was brought about between agriculture and
industry, a greater social homogeneity and indirectly
a deeper national feeling were created by the long-range
economic plan adopted by the Fifteenth Congress in
1928. Through the infernal years of 1928-1932 there
was cause for both exhilaration and discouragement in
the graphs of production. In several vital industries such
as coal, lumber, and steel, production fell below the
quotas set by the Planning Commission. Quality deterio-
rated with quantity to such a degree that in some instances nearly half of the manufactured product had to
be scrapped, while goods that reached the market were
often so poor that consumers refused to buy them despite
their scarcity. Yet with all the stumbling and muddling-
through, the country continued to make headway toward
its goals.

"To Catch Up and Outstrip America!" The goal
throughout the Soviet Union became "To Catch Up and
Outstrip America!" and to this end every means was
applied. No obstacle was regarded as sufficient to warrant
stoppage of work. The more portentous the international
outlook seemed, the more intense became the exertion of
the Soviet regime to achieve the colossal assignments.
"Complete the Five Year Plan in Four!" became the
slogan. A three-shift system kept industrial plants op-

erating around the clock. Bonuses reappeared, piecework and speed-up systems were introduced into every major plant. In 1935 a coal miner in the Donets Basin, A. Stakhanov by name, hit upon a plan which approximates the capitalist system known as Taylorism, with its time-and-motion methods for increased efficiency. He became the pacemaker, the Hero of Labor, a model of efficiency and a true son of the Socialist Fatherland. In the words of Stalin, Stakhanovism became "the expression of a new wave of socialist emulation." Special Stakhanovite teams or shock brigades, made up of the most efficient and skillful workers, were shifted hastily to every branch of industry where quotas showed signs of slumping or production was threatened with a breakdown. Absentee-ism was ruthlessly punished. By a decree of November 15, 1932, absentees without sound reason were not only expelled from their factories but deprived of their food rations. Nor was migration of workers tolerated: a pass-port system was restored in December 1932. By such harsh measures the government laid a foundation which enabled it to plan further "the building of socialism in a single country."

The Industrial Revolution. Although there were plenty of discrepancies between goals and achievements, still the achievements were impressive. Idle and untapped wealth throughout the Soviet Union was discovered and industrial enterprises established in formerly unknown or nonexistent communities. In the Ural District, for instance, the Solikamsk fertilizer plants went up. At Magnitogorsk, the Ruhr of Russia, where ore was being mechanically extracted, power plants and blast furnaces grew. At Karaganda and Kuznetsk coal basins were opened. At better-known centers such as Kharkov and Stalingrad great tractor factories were turning out equip-ment for mechanized agriculture. At Moscow ball-bearing and rubber plants were erected. New cities, notably Magnitogorsk in the Urals, sprang up like frontier gold-rush towns. Places which had been sleepy towns before the revolution grew within a few years into congested industrial cities: Stalinsk, Chelyabinsk, Stalingrad (later to be renamed Volgograd); Kramatorsk, an insignificant flag station in the Don Basin, by the end of the Second

Five Year Plan was turning out hoisting machines for mines and large quantities of equipment for twelve blast furnaces and for numerous rolling mills in western Siberia and iron and steel mills in the southern Ukraine.

On the eve of the war in 1941 the production of oil and steel had increased fourfold, that of coal sixfold. Automobiles and tractors, which prior to 1928 had virtually not been produced in Russia, were rolling off the conveyor belts. The Ford plant at Gorky and the Amo automobile industry at Moscow were the core of an automotive industry that in 1937 produced 200,000 cars and was scheduled by the end of the Third Five Year Plan to produce 400,000 annually. Even more impressive progress had been made in the truck industry. By 1937 the USSR was first in Europe and second in the world in the production of trucks. In the south the government was engaged in the construction of a huge power dam, the Dniprostroy. The chief foreign consultant was Hugh L. Cooper, an eminent American engineer. Begun in 1927, the dam was completed in 1932. Its annual production capacity of 2.5 billion kilowatt-hours surpassed all power generated in Russia prior to 1917. The dam raised the level of the Dnieper River, inundated the historic Dnieper Rapids, and made the stream navigable. By 1940 the USSR's electrical power output had risen to a total of 50 billion kilowatt-hours.

Much criticism has been showered upon the Soviet government for undertaking with such haste and callousness the industrialization of the nation. The plan no doubt was destitute of human feeling in its execution, and questions were at times raised whether it might not have been proper to moderate the tempo of industrial progress. To this Stalin repeatedly replied that the Soviet Union had alternatively to "perish or outstrip" the capitalist countries. (*See Reading No. 14.*)

The Five Year Plans were the lever with which the government pried the Russian people from their bed and set them in motion; they gave momentum to the masses to a degree that was destined to shape events for years to come. The nation was raised from a prolonged dormancy and made to realize its latent power. Only on the basis of this awakening can one find an explanation for the unleashed dynamism that enabled Russia to win the coming battles on the economic and later on the military front.

Furthermore, the accelerated program for industrialization was caused externally by the world situation and internally by the desire to avoid unemployment. It must be recalled that in Moscow the Locarno Pact was regarded with grave suspicion to alienate Germany from the Soviet Union and form a Western anti-Soviet bloc. Two years after the Locarno Pact, in 1927, several developments took place which further increased Soviet suspicions. In the West relations between the Soviet Union and Great Britain and France were severed while in the East the communist policy in China collapsed completely. Cumulatively there was every reason to believe that industrialization was most vital and absolutely necessary for national security.

— 5 —

THE THIRD
FIVE YEAR PLAN
AND AFTER, 1938-1953

Planning under the Shadow of War. The Seventeenth Congress of the Communist Party, which met in January 1934, urged certain revisions in order to increase the tempo of the Second Five Year Plan. The revisions called for further intensification of mechanization in industry, higher labor efficiency, superior quality of industrial products at lower cost, and greater volume of consumer goods for the famished domestic market. But the international situation did not permit the overlooking of heavy industry, which had to play a vital role in defense. This last consideration had been intensified by the time the Third Five Year Plan was announced in 1938. Then, under the imminent threat of war, greater attention had to be given to industrial plants from the Ukraine to eastern Siberia.

Science and labor were mobilized further to intensify exploratory work in search of minerals and oil deep in the interior. There was justified fear that the Caucasian oil fields were too much exposed: Baku lay at the border of Iran, Batum at the tip of the Soviet-Turkish frontier, and both were vulnerable to air attacks and invasion. To reduce the military danger the search for oil was urged while recently discovered fields west of the Urals were put into operation. The lower the clouds of war descended over eastern Europe, the less the attention to light industry was given. The hope that at last the masses would be compensated for the preceding barren years of industrial planning had to be abandoned. Reading 21 is a table which illustrates the supreme Soviet accomplishments as well as the aims of the Third Five Year Plan. (*See Reading No. 21.*)

As can be seen in the last column of this table, the targets for 1942 were interrupted by the outbreak of the war. The Third Five Year Plan therefore remained entirely unaccomplished. Even before the outbreak of hostilities military appropriations began to encroach increasingly upon industrial development. By 1941 military appropriations were nearly three times those of 1938. By the end of June 1941 the entire economy was in a turmoil caused by the Nazi invasion. There was no more time for setting lofty goals, only to fight for physical survival.

Sensing the oncoming holocaust the Third Five Year Plan from its very start stressed measures of national defense. Emphasis was laid on national transportation and steel, machine building, and chemical industries. Other metals, particularly nickel, zinc, aluminum, and lead, having military importance, were given equal priority. The Third Five Year Plan also included projects that provided for the improvement of electrification of certain railroads, double-tracking others, while in some part of the country entirely new railroads were to be constructed. Highways and water transportation were also taken into account. In western Siberia new sources of raw materials were to be tapped, notably aluminum and other nonferrous metals east of the Urals. There were new oil deposits to be opened east of the Volga, which the plan calculated would relieve the pressure upon the oil fields in the Caucasus.

Effects of the War. If heavy industry formerly took a high priority and left the consumer to occupy a low-priority place, in the Third Five Year Plan came a new tempo in investment in armaments and in conversion of industry into war production as never before. The effect was the same as during the first grim years of economic planning as far as the consumer was concerned—it left hardly 15 percent for consumption commodities. The rate of increase of industrial output was set at about 14 percent, a fairly low figure when compared particularly with the first few years of planned economy. Events soon proved that even this modest aim could hardly be realized; the Finnish war soon to be followed by the war with Germany reduced the plan to completely different goals—military victory at any cost. In terms of economic strength Germany, including the German-occupied areas in Europe, must have enjoyed a definite superiority. The decade of planning preceding the war was inadequate to conduct a conflict on a scale which was soon to stretch along a 1,700-mile frontier from the Arctic to the Black Sea. But the intangible factors that always enter in such circumstances were at first elusive: economists who measure opposing sides in sheer term of tonnage and output of "strategic materials" have badly miscalculated the strength of the opposing forces.

Inadequate though the economy of the nation was it proved that within the few years of planning the nation moved in the right direction. Some of the recently constructed industries were easily converted to war production, while the experiences of the preceding decade proved invaluable to more effective planning. The country managed to build up adequate stocks of vitally important materials such as zinc, bauxite, lead, and potash. With some difficulty the government managed to overcome the shortage in rubber, having already sufficient experience with synthetic rubber.

Far more serious was the shortage of such commodities as nickel, copper, tungsten, tin, antimony, and molybdenum. Equally serious was the inadequacy of certain industrial equipment, such as precision machine tools.

The element of surprise attack took its toll when in the winter of 1942 the Soviet Union had to roll back some 1,200 miles, all the way back to the Volga River. The inflicted economic damage was incalculable: recently built salient industrial centers as well as valuable agricultural areas were either laid waste or fell into the hands of the invading enemy. The government was stripped of the Ukraine, including the Donets Basin, and the northern Caucasus. Industrial cities such as Leningrad, Kharkov, and Stalingrad, despite a valiant defense, lost their industrial potential in the war effort. Coal, iron, steel, oil, these vital sinews of war were reduced in output between 60 and 70 percent, and agricultural produce was reduced about 35 percent.

According to some estimates the productive capacity of the Soviet Union had been lowered one-fourth. Although the main oil resources were saved from the invader, the loss of part of the northern Caucasus marked the loss of high-grade fuel. The interruption in the search for additional resources and the dispersal of scientists throughout the country was bound to affect the production of oil. Other industries were totally evacuated eastward; but by 1943 many of these, despite numerous difficulties, began to operate at full capacity. According to various estimates a total of 12 million persons were moved eastward from the invaded territories in the west. The burden this placed on passenger and freight traffic throughout the earlier part of the war can be easily imagined. The devastation was such that by the end of the war some 25 million people had been left totally homeless.

Postwar Economic Conditions. Following the Second World War the Soviet government came to face some towering tasks on the domestic front which demanded immediate attention. Demobilization was first on the agenda. In June 1945 the government took the first steps toward the gigantic undertaking: it ordered thirteen classes to be relieved from service, and provisions especially in regard to employment and housing were made for their return to civilian life. But the greatest of all postwar problems were the rehabilitation of the vast devastated areas formerly held by the enemy and the reestablishment of millions of displaced or disabled persons in life. According to official figures released by the Soviet government shortly after 1945, the war against Germany and Japan cost the nation 485 billion dollars, a sum equivalent to more than a six-year total of the Soviet national income. Of this sum 128 billion dollars was due to damages suffered from occupation or destruction by the invader. The destruction of property was listed as follows: 1,710 towns, 70,000 villages, 35,000 plants and factories, 40,000 hospitals, and 6,000,000 buildings, leaving some 25,000,000 citizens homeless.

Fifteen years later it was finally officially disclosed what perilous economic shoals the Soviet Union had reached by 1945. A special study by G. I. Shigalin entitled *National Economy of the USSR in the Period of the Great Patriotic War* reveals illuminating figures. Already at the end of 1942 Soviet heavy industry had suffered such losses that its level was at about that of the First Five Year Plan. Steel production in 1942 dropped about 60 percent—from 18.3 million metric tons* in 1940 to 8 million—coal from 165.9 million metric tons to 75.4 million.

Production of grain can be judged by the reduced area sown, dropping about 60 percent. The destruction of livestock in some cases reached most appalling conditions, as the following figures show:

	1941	1942	1943	1944
		(in millions of head)		
cattle	54.5	31.4	28.4	33.9
cows	27.8	15.0	13.8	16.5
pigs	27.5	8.2	6.0	5.6
sheep & goats	91.6	70.6	61.8	63.3
horses	21.0	10.0	8.1	7.7

* 1 metric ton equals 2,204.6 pounds.

Eugene Varga's Prediction. Many Soviet economists, as well as those in the West, predicted that the capitalist world would face a major depression after the war. The return to civilian life of millions of demobilized soldiers would result in mass unemployment and political unrest. But not all viewed the situation in this light. Among Soviet writers Eugene S. Varga stood out as one of the most prominent economists who did not agree with current views. In his publication entitled *Changes in the Economy of Capitalism as a Result of World War II,* which stirred quite a controversy, Varga made an effort at a reevaluation of the Communist ideology in terms of the reality of the capitalist world rather than in terms of how Marx saw the future a century before.

World War II had changed much in the field of economic affairs. Varga pointed out that the war had impoverished the continent of Europe, Japan, and China, whereas it had increased the productive power of the United States and Canada. He therefore predicted a postwar crisis of underproduction in the impoverished areas and of overproduction in North America. This minor crisis would be mitigated by a movement of economic aid from America to Europe and Asia. On this basis, concluded Varga, only when the impoverished countries had regained their prewar productivity—a process that would take at least ten years—would the real crisis of capitalism begin.

Another observation Varga made was that capitalistic states had assumed a decisive importance in the war economies. The necessity of a state to intervene in war production was not abandoned with the end of the war. This enhanced the role of the state permanently. Not all powers acquired by the state during the war were relinquished, or, if they were, experience taught the state to reinvoke them in the future in case of a major crisis. To drive home his contentions further Varga denied the common notion that under capitalism "anarchy of production" is the rule. The war taught these states to operate "state plans" which proved useful after the war. Volume of production, amount of export and import, all these are now planned with fair accuracy. Varga concluded the lessons of war taught capitalism to learn to plan and tame monopolists to work in the interests of the state. The world had changed, he concluded, and the philosophy of the Soviet system must change accordingly.

Varga instantly provoked many critics who denounced his interpretation of the world situation and downgraded him as an ideological theoretician and economic spokesman. His opponents claimed that he erred in measuring "impoverishment" in national rather than class terms. In all Western countries, his critics contended, despite the war ravages, monopolists emerged with increased wealth and power while the working classes were further pauperized, therefore only intensifying the class struggle. The Western states, they argued, by virtue of being capitalist, were incapable of planning a national economy. The monopolists of bourgeois states think only of earning profits. Instead of subduing their ravaging appetites they merely take over the state and subordinated the national interests to their own use.

Varga was equally criticized on political grounds. His thesis, the critics maintained, bore the stamp of wartime collaboration. During the war the main concern was defeat of Fascism and Nazism, whose aggression was aimed against Soviet as well as capitalist interests. After the war, the opponents argued, Varga failed to take into account the new nature of the struggle; he continued to romanticize bourgeois democracy and applied to it an alien doctrine of socialist planning. The naked truth however is that imperialist expansion continued and along with it followed the crushing of true democracy. This is the essence of postwar development which escaped Varga's analysis of the economic situation in the world. The period of tolerance must therefore come to an end and capitalism must cease to deceive Soviet leaders by lulling them into peaceful coexistence.

A storm of heated debates broke out in which the dogma of capitalist durability and avoidance of a total collapse was challenged. *Pravda*, organ of the Communist Party, severely took Varga to task for his belief "that a bourgeois state was capable of overcoming the spontaneous action of the law of value, the general law of capitalist accumulation and the law of pauperization of the working class; or that it was capable of overcoming depressions and unemployment—that it can become planned." It was only after the death of Stalin that Varga was "rehabilitated." Eventually his theories gained acceptance and his prediction that American economic credits would play an important role in the postwar world proved sound. The acceptance of Varga's interpretation meant for Russia an adoption of a policy that would keep pace with world economic developments.

The Fourth Five Year Plan. To bring national production in agriculture and industry back to prewar levels and to raise living standards was the immediate postwar aim of the Soviet government. For this truly mammoth task the Supreme Soviet of the USSR adopted on March 18, 1946, a Five Year Plan for the Recreation and Development of the National Economy of the USSR for 1946-1950. The undertaking contemplated no less than 205 billion rubles of industrial production by 1950. It called for a high rate of increase of iron and steel, coal, machinebuilding, food, and agrarian rehabilitation (a 27 percent increase by 1950 in the total farm produce); for a considerable program of expansion in the field of transportation and communications; and for the cultural advancement of the masses

In addition the Soviet government announced in October 1948 a fifteen-year conservation battle or reclamation plan involving some 300 million acres of land, affecting 80,000 collective farms. It was, according to the official announcement, "an offensive against drought, insuring final victory over the age-old enemy of agriculture." The plan called for prevention of soil erosion, reforestation, irrigation, fertilization, crop rotation and adaptation, and complete farm mechanization. The project represented a defense plan against the parching winds that blow from the Central Asian deserts and across the Caspian Sea. This involved the planting of forest belts of a total length of over 3,000 miles; it required the building of more than 45,000 reservoirs and artificial ponds which could be used either for irrigation or the manufacture of hydoelectric power. The main forest belts were plotted approximately thus: one from Saratov to Astrakhan; another one from Penza to Kamensk, on the Donets River; a third from Stalingrad (now Volgograd) to Kamyshin, along the Volga; a fourth belt from Chapayevsk, near Kuibyshev, to Vladimirovska; finally, the longest belt was to extend from the South Urals to the Caspian Sea at Gurev and from Voronezh to Rostov on the Don. This long-range planning called for huge investment capital; its success demanded political stability at home as well as abroad. The war-shattered economy once again called for extraordinary effort and a belt-tightening policy for peaceful advancement.

By the end of 1947 industrial output began to reach the prewar level. In some fields, such as steel and iron the rise in production was less spectacular; in others, such as light and textile industries, the recovery was much faster. In agriculture the year 1947 also showed a marked improvement. By the end of the year rationing was abandoned. At the same time a financial reform, replacing a new ruble for the old one, prevented chaotic conditions as a result of the termination of rationing. The new prices were higher to forestall an excessive demand of commodities. The currency conversion was mainly on a basis of 10 to 1 in cash holdings and 3 to 1 in war loan bonds.

Economic Situation in 1953. At the death of Stalin the economic situation in the Soviet Union was the result of a planned economy initiated a quarter of a century back. In agriculture the standard remained at a comparatively low level and necessary improvements at times lagged seriously. On the other hand notable progress was witnessed in industry, particularly heavy industry, largely due to the high-priority treatment it enjoyed. Throughout the Stalin rule heavy industry remained the favored child of Soviet economics and nothing was spared to stimulate its progress. The cost of Soviet industrialization was shockingly high, not only in terms of financial outlay but in blood and human toil. Even more shocking was the cost of collectivization, where peasant resistance was bitter, government determination to fulfill its set goals was unswerving, and the cost in lives tragic. The achievements in agriculture were far less spectacular than in industry. On the eve of Stalin's death the Soviet Union produced about 10 percent above 1914 totals. Priorities in agriculture as well as in wages remained at a low level, resulting in turn in low-quality produce, discrepancy in prices, and understandable discontent among the peasants.

In industry the situation looked quite different. By 1953 a notable shift in population took place from rural to urban centers, caused largely by the insatiable demand of industry for labor. On the other hand the surplus labor produced by collectivization and mechanization of agriculture made it possible for the countryside to supply the needed manpower in industry. During the twenty-five years of planned economy Soviet society had passed through notable changes: urbanization and industrialization made impressive strides. There was a growing class of skilled workers, of technocrats, and of scientists; and, combined, they all indicated the nature of the technological revolution that took place in the country. The Soviet Union was rapidly being transformed into an industrial power, competing, aspiring to overtake the industrial Western nations.

— 6 —

THE POST-STALIN YEARS

Immediate Successor of Stalin. Following the death of Stalin in March 1953, the premiership passed in rapid succession to Malenkov, then to Bulganin and Khrushchev, and then to Khrushchev alone. The shift was caused largely by conflicting views held among some of the most prominent Soviet leaders concerning industry and agriculture. During his thirty years in power Stalin had persistently followed a policy of priority for heavy industry. In a modern world, he believed, the chief source of state power was in its industrial capacity. In the field of agriculture Stalin adamantly followed the program originally set in the early 1930's of collectivization. The policy so doggedly followed by Stalin now came under serious reexamination.

Malenkov as Premier. Upon assuming the premiership Georgi M. Malenkov immediately faced a dual-natured task. One part was the need to relax tension in foreign affairs; the other concerned the conversion of industrial production to serve wider civilian needs. The termination of the war in Korea and the lessening need of arms production was an additional incentive to the pursuit of the peaceful policy Malenkov intended to follow. Above all, Malenkov believed, the time had come when attention should be turned by the state to the long-neglected Soviet consumer. As the first step in this direction an announcement was made on April 1, 1953, that the government had decided to lower prices on many consumer articles and food. Prices on meat were reduced 15 percent, footwear 8 percent, toilet articles 10 percent, women's apparel 14 percent, vegetables 50 percent, bread 10 percent. As an additional aid to the consumer the government reduced the compulsory purchases of state bonds by 50 percent. This left the consumers with a billion and a half rubles more to spend on articles they long wished to own. This did not yet assure the Soviet citizen of the sought commodities; the immediate effect was that the consumer found himself with more money to spend and an acute shortage of craved-for goods. Malenkov was therefore ready to take the next logical step.

Appearing before the Supreme Soviet in August he explained that though heavy industry must remain the backbone of the economy, conditions now made it possible for the country to increase the production of consumer goods. This, he said, was not only permissible, but urgently necessary, and for this reason he urged heavier investments in agriculture and in light industry producing consumer articles. Such a policy, he explained, would allow the public a greater abundance of foodstuffs and manufactured articles. This, he added, would entail the conversion of many industrial plants to mass production of consumer goods.

The pronouncement touched upon a subject that had

been lingering for some time but had been only lightly discussed as long as Stalin was ruling. Whereas the Stalinist line was to accentuate heavy industry as the single means and measure to power, Malenkov departed from this line and in so doing opened the dikes to a flood of criticism. He urged the government to focus its attention upon the consumer. The opponents argued that such a policy would invariably tend to undermine the national economy and the security of the state. Khrushchev labeled Malenkov's policy a distortion of Leninism and a return to the heresies of Bukharin. Khrushchev and his adherents won the political encounter though he later changed his view and even embraced some of Malenkov's recommended policies.

In the realm of agriculture Malenkov was prepared to introduce some changes too. One of the first things he proposed was to raise prices on farm produce, which would add greater incentives to production. He suggested that greater freedom be allowed the collective farmer in attending his private plot and determining prices on farm produce. Another step was to reduce farm income taxes and the amount of compulsory deliveries of garden produce to the state. The farmer, argued Malenkov, must be paid higher prices for his vegetables and dairy products or relieved in part of delivery quotas to induce greater production. He must be given greater freedom to sell more produce on the free market where he was able to get higher prices.

Malenkov Forced to Resign. Malenkov's proposals were not met with unanimous approval. His critics feared that he ran the risk of arousing unattainable expectations and pressure for concessions of incalculable ideological and political consequences. The party favored more caution and less haste. It is not without interest to note that though it was agreed in September 1953 to make some of the suggested concessions to the farmers, these were accompanied by a reaffirmation of the importance of party control, the firm hold upon the Machine Tractor Stations, and party organizations in the countryside. Though greater freedom was given the farmer to till his private garden, he was also given to understand that the collective land was not to be neglected. To make this even more specific, during the summer of 1954 the government made it abundantly clear once again that each member of the collective had to contribute a minimum of 300 workdays annually for every male and 200 for every female. Socialized farming was not to suffer from the recently granted freedom to till private plots.

The timing for Malenkov's agrarian program was rather unfortunate since it coincided with a number of annoying adversities. During the fall of 1953 the harvest showed a sizable drop compared with the previous year. To make things worse the following year the harvest showed little improvement. Such were the circumstances in which Malenkov had to bow out. His insistence upon greater priorities for light industry and consumer goods and his demand for a more liberal policy toward the peasantry led to his fall.

On February 8, 1955, Georgi M. Malenkov resigned his premiership. By his own admission, officially at least, he failed to solve the agricultural problem and decided to pass the premiership to someone better qualified to handle the critical problems. Malenkov's short-lived rule, despite his defeat, should nevertheless not be underestimated. For the first time since planned economy went into effect the interests of the consumer came up for a public airing; there were urgent demands, even though by a minority, for improvements in living standards of the Soviet citizen. The same could also be said about Malenkov's concern about agriculture. Finally, Malenkov's premiership can be regarded as the opening wedge in the forthcoming campaign against the "cult of the individual." This Khrushchev utilized more dramatically after he firmly established himself in power. The portentous expulsion of Beria from the party, followed by his execution in July 1953, marked the end of the Stalin era. In a broader sense the defeat of Malenkov marked the initial steps toward public recognition of the evils of Stalinism soon to be openly proclaimed.

Ascendancy of Khrushchev. Malenkov was succeeded by Nikolai Bulganin and Nikita S. Khrushchev as Premier and as First Secretary of the Communist

Party, respectively. The two, who commonly came to be referred to abroad as "B. & K.," introduced a novel practice of "collective responsibility," though not for too long, since Khrushchev soon assumed responsibility personally. There followed a period, until mid-1964, which commands special attention. Fashionable as it became shortly after Khrushchev's fall to refer to his policies as "harebrained schemes," history will be more charitable in evaluating his record, regardless of his failures in solving some of the problems he had to face or to cope more successfully with the daring ventures he frequently plunged into.

The Early Steps. Shortly after Khrushchev assumed sole mastery in the government a number of important changes were made in the management of the national economy, and others emanated indirectly from those introduced; vital economic issues came up for public discussions and fuller data were published soon after he took over the premiership. Throughout the Stalin regime the workers had no freedom to change employment. These rigid regulations were repealed in 1956. The eight-hour labor day was reduced to seven, while in industries hazardous to health and in mining it was shortened to six. A State Committee on Labor and Wages was engaged in a revision of wage scales and in adjustments to price levels and currency value; pensions were also increased. To add incentive for workers engaged in specially hazardous employment a separate wage scale was set for these. Wages for white-collar employees were also reexamined.

The labor unions, held inactive in the background while Stalin ruled, were now given greater recognition and allowed to express more openly their views concerning management, wages, and need of technical improvements.

The Sixth Five Year Plan, initiated in February 1956, was an attempt at a compromise between the advocates of heavy industry and the champions of the consumer. The plan aimed at an increase of 60 percent in the national income, 65 percent raise in industrial output and promised an increase of 30 percent in wages. But for several reasons by the end of 1957 the entire plan had to be revised. (*See Reading No. 22.*)

Year*	Housing Construction (in millions of square meters)	Year	Housing Construction (in millions of square meters)
1953	30.8	1957	52.0
1954	32.6	1958	71.2
1955	33.4	1959	80.7
1956	41.0	1960	82.8

* Cited in Harry Schwarz, *The Soviet Economy since Stalin* (Philadelphia: Lippincott, 1965), p. 82.

At the same time the ill-famed labor camps, associated with the rule of Stalin, were ordered to be closed and the inmates freed. During 1957 an expanded housing-construction program was put into effect with impressive results. The program included the use of standard-size, prefabricated materials, which greatly accelerated progress.

Industrial Management and Administration. The most noteworthy changes introduced by Khrushchev were in industrial management and administration. At the Twentieth Party Congress, Premier Khrushchev severely took to task industrial management for neglecting recent technological advances. Khrushchev took, as an illustration, the field of transportation, pointing out the failure to utilize diesel motors or electric power instead of continuing to use coal. Even more important, he denounced Stalinism and presented a grim record of purges, oppression, and the adulation of Stalin that commonly became known as the "cult of the individual."

The revolt in East Germany and Hungary stemmed in part from Khrushchev's castigations. By the end of 1956 the Soviet government came to face a number of unexpected difficulties in carrying out the Sixth Five Year Plan. A combination of circumstances led to an oncoming crisis: the Central Committee was given clear notice that additional 7 billion rubles for 1957 and 37 billion for the remaining five years would be required to attain the set goals. Furthermore, the same report also stated that the plan was being carried out with much waste, too high cost, and with considerable losses. The immediate answer was to name M. Pervukhin as head of the State Economic Commission in charge of current planning of the national economy as virtual dictator.

But Khrushchev was not to be satisfied with mere increase in authority of some head of a commission. In February 1957 he appeared before the Central Committee, where he insisted upon a total administrative overhaul. He attacked the prevailing slovenliness, waste, lack of rationalization, and, above all, senseless centralization in administering the Five Year Plan. To the surprise of everyone, above all of Pervukhin himself, the Committee took to heart Khrushchev's criticism and recommended decentralization and reorganization of the State Economic Commission, which the government had consolidated only three months before. Opponents such as Pervukhin, Molotov, Malenkov, and others were outvoted, and Khrushchev came out triumphantly when in May 1957 the Supreme Soviet approved the recommendation of the Central Committee. Within a matter of a few months the State Economic Commission passed from the highly centralized authority created in December 1956 to a decentralized one fashioned by the May 1957 action of the Supreme Soviet.

While still only first secretary of the party, Khrushchev also gained another political victory when under his urgent recommendation a plan was approved to expand in economic matters the authority of regional party leaders, reducing Pervukhin's authority further. Opponents of Khrushchev considered urging the removal of the first secretary of the party but failed. Among those who sought Khrushchev's removal evidently was no other than Bulganin himself, an act which sealed his political fate. Having managed thus far to carry out his program, Khrushchev began to feel master of the situation and acted accordingly.

Decentralization of Economic Administration. A complete reorganization of the economic administration now began. Twenty-five major economic ministries were completely abolished; those that survived the reform were mostly the ones engaged in the military program. Authority was now disseminated among 105 regional economic organizations, under the jurisdiction of the Councils of the National Economy, one for each of the fifteen constituent republics. In the national capital was the All-Soviet State Planning Committee, which was in charge of national planning and coordinating the work of the councils. The change was significant since it shifted much of the burden of responsibility upon the individual republics and the respective regional organizations. But the reorganization opened almost from the start several pertinent questions. One was the need to prevent the danger of "economic provincialism." There was an obvious danger of an excessive interest in purely regional or local interest in getting the utmost in industrial investment or in particularly favorite production at the expense of national planning. (*See Reading No. 23, where Djilas discusses planned economy; compare with Readings Nos. 30-32; 35-36.*)

Termination of the 1956-1960 Plan. Tampering with administrative reorganization in the midst of the five-year planning endangered the entire undertaking, the opposition warned. It was not long before the warning proved correct. Some vital industries began an ominous slowdown, mainly because of shortage of capital. By the fall of 1957 it became clear that the Five Year Plan required a total overhaul. Accordingly, in September it was announced that a new plan of longer range taking into account the new administrative changes was to be adopted. The Five Year Plan of 1956-1960 was thus terminated midway, presumably because the goals were set too high. The Hungarian revolt and the unrest in Poland during 1956, though not admitted, contributed further to the decision. A Seven Year Plan thus went into effect in 1958. (*See Readings Nos. 24-57.*)

Planning Transportation and Power in Siberia. To assure members of the Eastern bloc of regular and inexpensive oil delivery it became necessary to find other means of transportation than those formerly used. The long route running from Siberia was a serious handicap to the overburdened railroads. The difficulties were overcome by the construction of two pipeline systems, each more than 2,000 miles in length. The first, the Friendship Line, links the great Volga-Ural fields with the refineries of Poland, East Germany, Czechoslovakia, and Hungary. This line was completed with a delay of about a year because of a ban by NATO on shipments of large-diameter pipe from West German, Italian, and other Allied pipe mills to the Soviet Union. The second line extends from the Ural fields across Siberia to the Angarsk refinery near Irkutsk.

Of the two lines the former is of special importance since the increase in the flow of crude oil to the recently constructed refineries in Eastern Europe freed these member states of dependence upon the high-priced Western refined products. The line that extends from Kuibyshev on the Volga to Mozyr in Byelorussia, a distance of about 850 miles, is a 40-inch-diameter pipe. It was this line especially that was regarded by NATO as having military potential and caused the ban on pipe shipments.

In a crash program in the late 1950's the Soviet government expanded domestic pipe-making capacity. By the end of 1964 the entire project of the Friendship System was completed. One section reaches to the oil refinery of the Slovak capital of Bratislava; another branch extends into Hungary; a third serves the Polish refinery of Plock and the East German refinery at Schwedt.

The line from the Volga-Ural fields to Irkutsk is to serve domestic needs entirely with only possible potential export value in the future. The ultimate goal is to extend the line from Irkutsk to Nakhodka, a port on the Pacific. Most likely this project will depend on an agreement with Japan which would make Japan the main customer of Soviet crude oil. It involves a 28-inch pipe of about 2,500 miles in length. A line of this nature, it is contemplated, would be able to provide some 30,000 tons of oil daily, assuring Japan, Southeast Asia, and the countries bordering on the Pacific Basin a less expensive crude oil and freeing them from dependence upon the Western European countries and the United States.

A few months after Khrushchev's resignation Soviet transportation had accomplished another achievement by opening the long-projected 400-miles Siberian rail line, operating between Taishet, a key junction on the Trans-Siberian Railroad, and Abakan, on the Yenisei River. The Taishet-Abakan line had been under construction since 1958 in the terrain of one of the most underdeveloped, mountainous sections of southern Siberia. This filled a crucial gap in the Siberian transport system, linking the Trans-Siberian main line with a parallel line between Magnitogorsk and Abakan known as the South Siberian Railroad. The line is expected to serve a twofold purpose of opening up the mineral-rich Sayan Mountains and shortening the haul between Siberian steel plants and their coking coal and iron-ore suppliers.

Ever since the First Five Year Plan was initiated efforts were exerted to shift the hub of Soviet industry eastward. During the 1950's the policy had continued to industrialize Siberia on a continental scale. This has been demonstrated particularly with the construction of the Bratsk power station. The dam will have a capacity of 4.5 million kilowatts—twice that of the Grand Coulee dam.

The dam is located near the town of Bratsk, located on the shores of the manmade sea about twenty miles above the dam. Along the shores are rapidly rising other industrial settlements. Together these will eventually form the Bratsk complex, which will include huge aluminum, wood pulp, and cellulose and chemical plants that will produce fertilizers, plastics, and fibers, as well as a steel mill. The development is bound to transform the Siberian wilderness, clear the forest primeval or "taiga," and change the familiar face of that country.

Termination of the Seven Year Plan. The fate of the Seven Year Plan was similar to the one that preceded it. On March 13, 1963, the government dropped this plan, two years before the set date for its completion. This time the reason given was that the situation had been so drastically changed since 1958 that the plan as originally conceived called for radical alterations. Technological changes along with administrative and managerial reforms, presumably, compelled the government to bring the plan up to date.

The new plan was to take into account the new regional organizations and was assigned to a Supreme Council of National Economy, a body similar to the one that functioned between 1917 and 1932. This council was to include a special committee for space planning and other agencies. In the field of agriculture several agencies were formed to take charge of modern agricultural machinery, chemical fertilizers, and research and development in marketing of produce. The plan incorporated as well research into the raising of standards of living, bettering housing facilities, and related problems. The ambitious plan was to be carried out by 1970.

The Virgin Lands Venture. On the "agricultural front" the picture had been somewhat dimmer, showing far less spectacular records than in industry. Here weather conditions, despite all mechanization, remained of decisive importance, while human error at times added devastating results to the economy. The road to costly failure in the bold adventure of Khrushchev was truly paved with his best of intentions. In search for more adequate supplies to feed an increasingly urbanized and industrialized society, Khrushchev had decided that Soviet agriculture must derive a higher yield per acre by way of utilizing chemical fertilizers, that the cultivation of corn was to be increased, and that vast tracts of idle land in Central Asia was to be opened to farming. To impress the Russian farmers Khrushchev traveled more miles, delivered more speeches, made more trips abroad, and committed more promises than any previous Soviet leader. (*See Reading No. 29.*)

On the surface Khrushchev's solution was as simple as it was sound. Here were vast areas of promising land that could be utilized within a matter of a few years. Equipped with modern agricultural machinery, scientific means, and trained personnel this land could be converted into a gigantic producing area that would supply the badly needed produce and even provide grain for export.

The program promised a minimum of 50 percent increase in the grain crop. Khrushchev was firmly optimistic in his views despite some discouraging counsel to take into consideration the fact that this marginal land was grazing land located in areas often exposed to severe droughts. The only fact that disturbed Khrushchev somewhat was the sparse population on this land. But this did not deter Khrushchev, for it was soon announced that thousands of tractors, combines, and other modern machinery would be dispatched to put into operation the projected grain factories. Simultaneously an appeal was issued to young people to "Go Eastward" where golden opportunities awaited them and their country.

The Great Gamble. Khrushchev's project was a gigantic gamble; it was an original scheme though an expensive one. Within two years no less than 87 million acres were put to the plow. About a half of this newly cultivated land was in Kazakhstan. Inspired by the cornfields of Iowa and Kansas, Khrushchev now began to have visions of similar cornfields on an even vaster scale than those he observed in the American Middle West. In vain did some experts try to dissuade Khrushchev, arguing that Kansas corn could hardly be cultivated in Russia, where shorter seasons would not permit the crop to ripen.

By 1960 approximately 70 million acres were given to the raising of corn. Such a vast crop, it was believed, would help to increase the production of meat and livestock no less than 100 percent. Corn would render fodder and thereby aid in saving grain for human consumption. Furthermore, much of the virgin lands could also be used for cultivation of wheat. By 1958 nearly 50 million acres were given to wheat raising. Estimates show that the investment in this project exceeded one billion dollars. Some 350,000 young Russians moved to Central Asia along with thousands of students who went to work during the summer vacations.

The years from 1956 to 1958 seemed encouraging, since rainfall proved adequate and the yield was promising. The year 1958 yielded an exceptionally good harvest and Khrushchev began to visualize the flowing prosperity he had predicted. Optimism carried away the planner who now anticipated an even higher yield during the next year. This hope was soon dashed when the crop of 1959 showed a drop of some 15 percent. It was a disheartening experience. The immediate effect was a shortage of forage, which in turn caused a drop in production of meat.

For three years there followed a consistent decline in grain production, from 14.3 million metric meters in 1958 to 10.1 in 1962. A year later Premier Khrushchev had to announce that the 1963 harvest was 20 percent below the one of last year and that therefore the Soviet Union was compelled to import grain from abroad. The crop failure not only affected the cereals but many essential vegetables, eggs, meat, and other products. Because the wheat-crop failure was attributed in part to shortages in fertilizers, there was a firm resolve to abandon the previous policy of expanding acreage by plowing virgin lands and instead a policy of raising farm output by increasing yields on the already-filled lands by means of fertilizers and irrigation.

The frequent droughts that parched the lands of Central Asia, the exhaustion of the grazing lands caused by intensive cultivation, which quickly reduced its fertility, and the failure to rotate crops intensified the failure. Plowing, accompanied by hot winds, caused the loss of whatever moisture there was in the soil. Further damage was inflicted by the blowing away of the valuable top soil and erosion of the area. What this amounted to in the end was a double loss—the experience failed to produce the planned crops and simultaneously prevented the utilization of the area as grazing land, thereby reducing the meat production. To this may be added the loss of major capital investment which could have been turned into more profitable use in other areas. All in all the virgin lands program ended in a complete fiasco.

Admission of Failure. On March 9, 1964, marking the tenth anniversary of the virgin lands program, the government with some difficulty was able to find dubious consolation in the failure it witnessed. The plowing, it was stated, rendered valuable lessons to the country by emphasizing the urgent need of an irrigation plan and intensive cultivation by way of utilizing chemical fertilizers even in the fertile areas of the country. Had an irrigation project preceded the opening of the Central Asian lands, the drought effect would not have had the devastating result that it did. By 1964 the Soviet Union had presumably the most up-to-date atomic-warhead missiles, hydrogen bombs, orbital devices, and unmanned cosmic stations, yet the government had to buy 12 million tons of wheat abroad to feed an undernourished population. Still Khrushchev lost no courage and held out promise that as crop yields increased in the more fertile areas, as expanded irrigation plans were completed, and the use of chemical fertilizers applied, the virgin lands would be restored to grazing once again.

Admitting serious failures, Khrushchev was not ready to surrender. This time the answer to the encountered difficulties was, according to Khrushchev, that as in the days of Lenin Communism meant Soviet power plus electrification of the Soviet Union, so now Soviet power plus chemistry meant triumph. Accordingly, a project was presented filled with endless figures, accompanied by data pertaining to crop yields, application of chemical fertilizers, and comparative figures, and, finally, pledges that a new page was to be turned in the history of the Soviet Union that would be entitled the "Chemical Era."

"The Chemical Era." Because production in agriculture had been lagging, barely keeping up with the population increase and becoming worse with the poor harvest in 1963, by the end of the 1950's Khrushchev began to regard the chemical industry as the answer to many disturbing economic difficulties. The plan remained on paper as the metal industries continued to hold high priority. It was only in December 1963 that he revived his plan that was to open bright hope for the nation— the plan declared that the road to affluence was chemistry!

Synthetics, contended Khrushchev, would provide footwear and clothing more reasonably priced; multicolored plastics would adorn houses, and the supply of foodstuffs would be forthcoming in greater volume and higher quality. By 1970 chemistry would be instrumental in building an industry of abundance, opening limitless possibilities, trebling national production, and quadrupling fertilized output. A multitude of fertilizer-grown foods were envisioned. A vigorous campaign was opened with an outpouring of all kinds of publications in the popular sciences, mostly in chemical processes.

The magnitude in the manufacturing capacity of farm chemicals consisting of fertilizers based on nitrogen or phosphorus was staggering. Equally impressive was to be the production of different kinds of insecticides and herbicides: synthetic resins, plastics, artificial rubber, and fibers for the output of clothing and plastic for shoemaking. The national needs ran into millions of tons of fertilizers annually for several years. It has been estimated that the increase of production alone would be equivalent to half of the entire United States fertilizer industry, not to mention the wide range of chemical synthetic products and plastics.

In a four-hour speech before the Central Committee of the Communist Party, Khrushchev held out expectations rising from the enormous improvements that had been achieved and those to be derived from the forthcoming changes recommended; and the Central Committee supported the project. This demanded an enormous capital investment of about 46 billion rubles for the next seven years, 1963-1970, an allotment twice as much as the Soviet government invested in chemicals since 1917. This truly staggering sum provided for modernization of the entire chemical industry, the construction of more than 200 new plants and the expansion of about 500 factories already in operation. It required enormous imports of machinery, mostly from the United States, Great Britain, and France, and to a lesser degree from Japan and Italy. A plan of such magnitude could not be carried out on the existing basis of short-term credits: it demanded long-term credits and time payments.

Long-Term Credits: United States and Great Britain. The greatly increased program of investment in chemicals in the Soviet Union, as was pointed out, had led to a demand for specialized equipment that either could not be supplied by the Soviet industry or could be much more quickly supplied from abroad. The United States consistently and steadfastly kept adhering to a policy of no extension of credits to any Communist country for more than five years, since this would amount to foreign aid, frowned at by the members of NATO. Furthermore, the United States regarded the extension of credit terms to allow the Soviet Union to weather the economic crisis it was experiencing as inconsistent with its national interests: it would inadvertently assist Moscow in the maintenance of nuclear armament production. The attitude of the United States was perhaps best demonstrated during the Chemical Fair held in Moscow in September 1965. While Great Britain, France, Italy, Japan, and West Germany had massive displays of their chemical industries, the United States had only a small display of consumer goods made from chemicals in the Union Carbide pavilion. The fair reflected the increasing role played by all countries, with the exception of the United States, in supplying chemical equipment to the Soviet Union's expanding industry. As the Soviet government kept funneling ever-greater shares of its investments into chemical development, foreign nations in various degrees became involved in one or more major construction projects.

Though timidly, Britain was the first to demonstrate an interest in the Soviet program. In November 1964 a Soviet mission sent to London signed a preliminary, nonbinding contract. The largest project of the contract involved a 40-million-pound investment in a plant to produce Terylene, a synthetic textile fiber. Plants for other chemicals, such as synthetic rubber and acetic acids, were bid for by other companies. Several clearing banks were involved in the negotiations with the companies to finance these contracts. The British government's Export Credit Guarantee Department had offered credits of up to a total of 95 million pounds for periods of ten to fifteen years.

This did not please Washington, but the United States government was given to understand by Great Britain that London had no intention of waging economic warfare with the Communist countries over long-term credits for the Soviet Union. Britain had always opposed moves to restrict East-West trade except in the fairly rigidly defined strategic goods and had especially criticized the extension of the list of such goods. Great Britain, as the world's largest importer of primary products, regarded the Soviet Union as well as the Soviet bloc as a potentially useful area to trade in. It came to the opinion that the Eastern European countries could not be neglected, particularly since the exclusion of Britain from the Common Market. A somewhat similar view was held by Italy, Japan, and particularly France.

Long-Term Credits: France. An even bolder attitude was taken by France, thereby breaking completely the tradition of the five-year limit determined by the Berne convention on credit to Eastern European states. A five-year trade agreement was signed on October 30, 1964, between France and the Soviet Union. The agreement provided 356 million dollars in credits to the Soviet Union for seven years. On the part of France it was an effort to expand her markets in Eastern Europe and establish cooperation with the Soviet Union. The agreement was to go into effect from 1965 through 1969.

The Franco-Soviet trade agreement called for an exchange of products valued at 1.44 billion dollars, an increase of some 60 percent in trade between the two nations. Of this amount approximately 840 million dollars was earmarked for French export to the Soviet Union and about 600 million dollars Soviet export to France. The greatest advantage of the agreement as far as France was concerned was the provision to triple the sale of capital goods to the Soviet Union compared with exports under the trade pact preceding the October 1964 pact. The agreement mentioned specifically the construction of plants for the manufacture of chemical fertilizers, synthetic rubber, petrochemical products, and paper and wood products. The French were also to sell machinery and other equipment for Soviet industry. In exchange, France agreed to raise her annual purchases of Soviet crude oil from 550,000 tons to 1,830,000 tons and of refined oil from 875,000 tons to 915,000 tons.

The contracting parties also agreed that both would exert all efforts to increase exchange of agricultural products.

The Soviet chemical program was of such scope that foreign capital and import of machinery as provided by the trade agreements was still inadequate. Aside from the construction of physical plants the "chemical era" involved the promulgation of vital legislation. The plan called for the training of a legion of new technicians and engineers for the chemical industry. The educational system was by no means prepared for the formidable changes involved. The program was bound to call for more pedologists, farm chemical departments, agricultural chemists, and an increase in chemical research in the academies and universities. The program had to reach out into secondary education, and it prompted the introduction of a study in the field of chemistry where it was formerly omitted, demanding a major revision of the high school curriculum.

A chemical industry had operated in the Soviet Union for some time, but was woefully inadequate for the newly conceived operation and its utilization in agriculture. The industry had formerly been given low priority and was far behind the recent advances in the production of synthetic resins, fibers, and plastics. Though Soviet chemists had experimented quite early with synthetic rubber, largely because of difficulties in obtaining natural rubber from abroad, the industry made slow advances. There was little done in synthetic footwear, in clothing, in consumer goods, and in a variety of other articles familiar in the West. This Khrushchev decided to correct, though agricultural needs were still given the highest place on the priority list.

The chemical development program would require a total reallocation of investment resources to provide for a rapid construction of plants and greater output of fertilizers and numerous sophisticated products of modern chemistry. Above all, it required curtailment of the military budget. Whether it would be possible to cover the enormous military needs and simultaneously provide for the planned expansion of the chemical industry was uncertain. It was realized that the chemical program as planned was also bound to affect the consumer and delay projected raises in wages which had been promised in 1962 and postponed until 1965. The diversion of resources to the chemical program would cut back in many other areas of the economy, such as in new plant construction in the iron steel industry.

Libermanism. The question of labor and management efficiency had been a recurrent subject of discussion as well as of government concern for some time in the Soviet Union. Soviet factories operated on orders from a centralized planning agency. The consumer was of little consideration as to either need or taste; the basis for judgment was mainly the volume or the ability of a plant to fulfill the quota set from the centralized planning office. The central planning system recognized one criterion—fulfillment of the production plan.

In recent years the fallacy of the system was best demonstrated by the staggering amount of defective and unwanted articles in government stores. During 1964 deliveries of 257 factories had to be suspended because their goods would not be purchased. Furthermore, state trade organizations returned or marked down 20 percent of all clothing, 10 percent of hosiery, and 9 percent of shoes produced. There were endless complaints about many other articles, including radios, televisions, washing machines, and refrigerators. The stiffening of the consumer in his demand for quality in the items he purchased and the increased number of protests resulted in some millions of dollars worth of unsalable items accumulated in Soviet inventories that no one wished to buy despite their great need. This glut also indicated the need not only of higher quality merchandise but of production quotas to be patterned to the needs of the market instead of arbitrarily set state plans. All told it indicated with increasing clarity that a formidable force of popular pressure was to be recognized, a demand to honor the desire of the people for more and better consumer goods.

Great difficulties also stemmed from a policy of paying bonuses to plant and factory managers who were able to carry out or exceed their assigned quotas of production. Bonuses were paid on the basis of quantity and time of delivery. This was no longer acceptable since under the pressure of the consumer there began a shift of emphasis, from pursuit of quantity to an accent on quality. There has been more and more frequent demand for a system whereby a worker's output would be paid according to the quality of excellence and satisfaction, while deduction would be made for poor work.

Furthermore, in some industries such as footwear and apparel, a system would be introduced according to which the factories would plan their output on the basis of goods actually sold; consumer tastes would be the determining factor rather than a central plan. Accordingly, factories would plan production on the basis of the store orders and factory performance would be judged on the basis of the consumers' approval of the commodity in question—the approval or disapproval of the shopper would determine the success or failure of the product. Such was in essence the profit-incentive system recommended for the industry by Yevsey G. Liberman. A change to "Libermanism" involved a vastly complex task of revamping the entire planning and operating structure of the economy opposed by the traditional economists and other vested interests.

Yevsey G. Liberman, Professor of Economics at the University of Kharkov, had devoted much of his study to the problems of industrial management and efficiency. He came to the realization that the Soviet economy has become too complex and sophisticated to be handled by a single centralized bureau. He diagnosed the malady as the "cult of the plan." In September 1962 he published his *Plan, Profit and Bonuses,* which initiated a nationwide debate. It was a more refined presentation of a theme Liberman had presented in an article in the magazine *Kommunist* in which he recommended that industrial efficiency and quality could be improved by greater emphasis on profitability.

Liberman was among the first to detect the true weaknesses in the Soviet economy and managerial system: the emphasis on turnout quantity of a product and time of delivery rather than quality standard; the disregard of the consumer as a determining element in production; the methods resorted to by industrial managers to gain assignments derived from the former two fallacies. Industrial managers usually exerted all efforts to win assignments that required lowest quantity and least sophisticated processes to produce the ordered commodities. Managers had no choice in defining the nature of the materials involved, the labor methods employed, or the possible reduction in cost or the profit percentage. All these matters were predetermined from the central planning agency above.

To correct the situation Professor Liberman suggested that profit be made the prime element. "The higher the profit, the greater the incentive," to both efficiency and quality. He urged that planning decrees be replaced by contracts between government and enterprise, with the lowest bidder getting the particular job and setting its prices as a result. He insisted that managers be given complete freedom in choosing assignments. Managers themselves should judge which assignments they were also able to carry out best and most efficiently. Each manager should be able to choose the resources to produce the articles he had contracted to deliver and the labor methods he thought would be most advisable to employ. Lastly, rather than awarding bonuses to managers for speed of delivery alone, payments should be based on the rate of profit earned on total capital invested in the production. The higher the rate of profit the enterprise gained, the higher the bonus should be. The Liberman plan could be considered as some kind of a profit-sharing procedure which would provide a principle—the better the quantity of the output, the higher would be the income of the factory, in which case the better would be the worker's pay. It was only logical to deduce from this that once profit became the basic principle, prices would have to respond to the market forces of supply and demand instead of being determined by the centralized authority of a planning board.

The practical effects of the plan are as follows. If merchandise is of inferior quality or out of style the stores have the right to return it to the factory. Before long the factory would face a decline in orders. This in turn is bound to reduce the profits of the factory and result in a proportionate decline in workers' bonuses. The result would be a rising awareness among the workers themselves of a need of higher quality work and an incentive to produce improved articles. In the late fifties experiments with the profit motive were carried out; by the early sixties the idea seemed to have passed from the experimental stage to the more widespread use.

Western observers were quick to deduce that by resorting to the heretical capitalistic profit motive, which is incompatible with Marxist doctrine, the Communist economy had acknowledged that it had failed. In short, capitalism began to rear its ugly head in the Soviet economy. Liberman and his followers hastened to warn these economists that they were in total error to assess Soviet emphasis on profits as a return to capitalism. The Communist ideology, Liberman contended, remained as before and the profit motive was merely a Western economic device which proved more practical, and nothing more; it had been applied long before Liberman came to advocate it. Profit, Liberman maintained further, was never denied in the Soviet Union. "Denial of profit by socialism and recognition of profit by capitalism," argued Liberman, "has never served as the feature distinguishing socialism. The difference is in the way profit is formed, appropriated and used." *

Profit, added the followers of Liberman, was never the sole purpose of production, but was only to improve and expand production, while under a planned economy profit serves to show the efficiency of the methods employed. Some see in profit the index of assessing or encouraging progress in Soviet industry. This, however, should not be interpreted as any intention of the Soviet system to relinquish centralized planning management. Libermanists believed that the profit system they advocated must only ensure a better economic system carefully planned by a national board and free of crises. Contracts between individual enterprises and a centralized planning board on the outlined profit basis would not be the products of erratic market fluctuations, but fulfillment of a carefully adopted pattern of economic development. Therefore Libermanism was not an anti-

* *Time*, February 12, 1965.

Communist panacea, but a remedy to make Communism more efficient.

Nevertheless the appearance of the profit motive in the Soviet economy was bound to carry with it long-range political implications. Some thought that the weakening of the centralized planning machine was bound to lead to a similar weakening of the party grip over the economy. Formerly shackled local initiative was bound to gain self-assurance and demand recognition in other fields.

The application of the profit principle had been tried out officially in a restricted area as a test. Two clothing factories in Moscow and Gorky were permitted to negotiate prices and sell their merchandise directly to 22 retail stores. The stores instructed the factories as to the kind of merchandise the consumers demanded. The two factories became the focus of national attention. Here management was geared to making a profit instead of merely fulfilling specified quotas. Workers' bonuses depended entirely upon the profits the enterprises made. The results had proved most encouraging: costs were reduced, industrial efficiency raised, and quality, under pressure of the consumer, improved. In some cases profit margins gave workers an income of 15 to 20 percent above their basic pay rate. The experiments at the Moscow and Gorky factories proved so successful that early in 1965 some 400 clothing and shoe firms and 78 of their raw-material suppliers throughout the Soviet Union were permitted to change to the new system. The loosening of centralized planning controls went step by step, soon extending to the machine-building industry, one of the key sectors of the Soviet economy. The extension of autonomy to the machine-building industry meant that factories would have the right to place orders directly with supplier plants for needed equipment without having to send their requests through cumbersome government machinery.

There was some hesitancy but the press prodded the government and insisted upon "bold decisive action" in the national economy in order to attain success. On August 17, 1964, an article appeared in *Pravda,* the Communist Party organ, signed by Academician Trapeznikov, in which the author asked for a special commission to study the problem of industrial management. This relaunched the debate about the proper role of profits in a planned economy, and the discussion quickly gathered momentum and was carried on in other papers. Professor Liberman stepped in once more to argue in favor of profits as the main criterion of efficiency. He reiterated that for this criterion to be generally applicable the rate of profits should be related to firms' "productive capital," and that for the sake of productivity there should also be a link between profits and wages. If prices are sufficiently flexible, argued Liberman, and calculated not centrally but by regions and local branches, it should be possible to give much more freedom to individual firms within the general planned framework. The search for profits, contended Liberman, was found to force each firm to increase production, raise quality standards, and introduce new techniques.

Professor Liberman challenged once more Western writers who hastily concluded that the Soviet Union was moving toward a market economy and free enterprise. Profits, Liberman argued again and again, cannot play the same part in the Soviet economy as they do in capitalist countries. The main reason for this is that in the Soviet Union profits cannot be turned into private capital to obtain ownership of the means of production. Nor can the system of profit in the Soviet economy undermine central planning. On the contrary, here the suggested reforms were bound only to improve planning because the authorities would no longer have to waste time on the details of control. (*See Reading No. 33.*)

The Fall of Khrushchev. During his term of office Khrushchev had managed to compile an impressive record of achievement which even his appalling failures do not obliterate. His bold attack on the Stalin cult, his formulation of a "peaceful coexistence" policy and denial of the inevitability of war, his space program, and his handling of Titoism will remain among his outstanding achievements. Less successful was his struggle with centralized administration and entrenched bureaucracy. (*See Readings Nos. 20-22.*) The Soviet industrial hierarchy still remained a stubbornly complex and often

cumbersome setup. (*See Readings Nos. 23-25.*) Through
all the changes, shifts, and reorganizations, major and
minor, so frequently undertaken, the hierarchy proved
dishearteningly unshaken. When we turn to Khrushchev's
economic program, including his agricultural policies,
here the record is even more daring but far less successful
in accomplishment. And it is the latter that largely contributed to his fall.

The year 1964 showed a definite slowdown in the rate
of economic growth. This is largely explained by the decline of labor productivity. The decline was frequently
caused by workers wandering off in search for new jobs
and higher wages or better labor conditions. This in turn
affected living standards which Premier Khrushchev tried
so hard to raise during his entire term of office. Statistical
data reveal that by the end of the third quarter of 1964
industrial productivity rose no more than 4 percent over
the period of the preceding year, while during the same
months of 1963 the growth showed 6 percent. Industrial
growth during the first six months of 1964 was the slow-
est since 1940.

Libermanism was still only beginning to be applied and
still had no chance of showing any appreciable effect
upon national production, nor did it even receive yet its
official blessings for national application. The 1964 decline in productivity is largely explained by the 1963
harvest failure, discontent over living conditions, frequent search for better jobs, and the impact of the poor
harvest upon the food processing industry. In part the
decline could also be explained by the recent priority
given to capital investment in chemical production while
other programs had to be curtailed. Cuts were made in
such branches as steel, iron, and machine-tool industries.
Overtaking the United States still remained as distant a
hope as ever.

Rise of Opposition against Khrushchev. There began to appear in the press some serious misgivings about
Khrushchev's ability to cope with the complex issues he
came to face. There were some accusations about his
"subjective" handling of some of the problems, his "drifting" which resulted in downward trends in the rate of

growth. *Pravda* came out eventually with a blunt statement, labeling Khrushchev's economic gyrations "harebrained scheming, immature deductions, and hasty decisions and actions divorced from reality, bragging and phrasemongering." Under fire came especially his advocacy of the corn-hog economy and his boasting to out produce the United States in meat and dairy products in the early 1960's. It was the virgin lands program that was referred to as his "harebrained scheme." Khrushchev's refusal to consider the opinion of scientists on the danger of plowing up the grasslands was another reason for the attack. He was reminded of his "harebrained idea" of planting sugar beets, peas, fodder beans, and other high-protein crops instead of retaining the tracts of land for fodder grasses. The critics now reminded Khrushchev of his humor when he said that his dispute with the scientists would be arbitrated more authoritatively by the cows. Data concerning production of livestock are scarce, indicating that the situation was becoming serious. There was an alarming decline in the number of cattle and pigs.

The clearest indication of the serious plight of agriculture was already revealed in September 1963 when by agreement with the Canadian government the Soviet Union purchased 228 million bushels of wheat. For centuries Russia has been one of the main wheat-producing nations in the world, annually exporting considerable quantities. It is not clear whether the shortage of wheat was the result of natural adversities or the faltering agricultural policies of the government. Critics of Khrushchev maintained upon the latter, apologists consider the former as the reason for the unfortunate development. Very likely it must have been a combination of both that ended with the need to import grain. Wherever the cause lies, the fact remains that the Soviet-Canadian agreement was a serious blow to the prestige of Khrushchev and contributed to his fall. Opponents of Khrushchev were unable to digest the fact that whereas in the United States wheat production reached the highest yield per acre ever and was producing twice as much wheat as the country needed, ending with 1,200,000,000 bushel surplus, the Soviet government had to seek wheat abroad to feed its population. It must have been a painfully humiliating experience to look at such statistical data.

There were other criticisms, such as the frequent changes in forms of management. Khrushchev's frequent shifts from centralization to decentralization, then later once more to centralization of agricultural management, as an illustration, came under severe attack. His adoption of plans on the spur of the moment, without proper consultation, involving the establishment of numerous agencies specializing in crops such as corn, sugar beets, cotton, and potatoes all indicated his bewilderment with the complexity of the agricultural problem and confusion in solving it. Khrushchev planned to convene the central committee of the party in November 1964 to consult the important party members, but his ideas were already formed with little chance to discuss them in detail. He was prepared to have his comrades state their views, but was equally ready to defend his schemes and see that they were carried out, and then "let the cows arbitrate." He had endless solutions ready to be applied on short notice regardless of consequences. As one critic observed, he had numerous schemes and few solutions. By the middle of October 1964 the Khrushchev era had come to an end. At a dramatic session of the party presidium, it was announced, Premier Khrushchev had resigned both his governmental and party posts.

To what extent the fall of Khrushchev was brought about by straight opposition to the policies he pursued is not clear. There were opponents of Khrushchev who believed that he was "soft on capitalism," evidently having in mind his policy of coexistence and willingness to face a break with the Chinese—a schism in the Communist world—for the sake of an understanding with the West. There were those who stressed the faults and weaknesses of the domestic situation, which only added further strain and stress and invigorated Khrushchev's critics. Whatever the immediate cause, it was a combination of long-standing causes that in the end resulted in the formation of a formidable coalition of opponents. Broadly speaking the fall of Khrushchev was brought by his foreign policy which proved unsuccessful in reducing military expenditures and internal economic difficulties which prevented him from keeping his pledges to the consumers.

Khrushchev's policy of coexistence failed to deliver domestic dividends. But above all stood out the farming disasters which damaged his reputation as the benefactor of the masses. Khrushchev was clearly aware of this and tried desperately to restore his reputation by endless changes in policy and new promises of increased output of consumer goods and improvement in agriculture. In the end many of these shifts came too frequently and too late to save him. It increased the hostility among the military men who were troubled by thoughts about the "missile gap" as well as antagonized party members who became weary of economic trial-and-error policies. As is usual, once an opposition decides to dispense of a leader it never fails to pinpoint his faults. He was criticized for his excessive oratory, for his impulsiveness, his garrulousness, irresponsibility, and, of all things, for his creation of a "Khrushchev cult." To the more sophisticated men of the younger generation Khrushchev's manners seemed a bit too crude and his "goulash" philosophy primitive. Yet he was accepted for more than a decade as the symbol of change, a champion against Stalinist cult of personality.

Agriculture, Underlying Cause of Khrushchev's Fall. Khrushchev's failure to cope with the serious agricultural problems was his biggest liability. Here Khrushchev applied all his ingenuity and found no satisfactory answer. Early in 1964 he came upon a new plan, to combine collective and state farms into regional producing and marketing associations. Each association would be in charge of the assigned area, with the entire inventory that belonged to the state under its single management. The advantage of such an organization, Khrushchev believed, would be a more effective way of handling all involved activities during the harvest time, including operating small-scale industries for processing farm products and taking charge of materials necessary for local needs. This would eliminate the duplication in the separate functions of some 40,000 collective and 8,500 state farms.

Closely connected with the cause of the decline of

Khrushchev's popularity was the consumer. Though not a decisive factor in the fall of Khrushchev, the consumer must have had an indirect effect. It was only in October 1964 that Premier Khrushchev belatedly announced that the Soviet government planners were requested to draw up plans that would provide priorities to satisfy "the material and spiritual needs" of the mass consumers. The request was a novelty, since the planners were never officially requested to give priority to the need of the consumer. Malenkov tried this in 1953, a few months after the death of Stalin. He initiated a short-lived economic principle which centered upon the consumer goods as the "fundamental basis" of the Soviet economy. The effort was unsuccessful and contributed to his fall.

Morally Khrushchev was committed to the reorientation of Soviet economic goals, and since 1957 he had committed himself on several occasions. In that year he promised the Russian people that within three years they would consume as much meat annually as the United States. In 1960 he held out hope that income tax would be abolished. On several other occasions he pledged an economy of abundance in this generation. And still living standards remained the same or showed too slow an improvement. Increased contacts with the West and a better acquaintance with Western standards of living further necessitated improvement in the lot of the Soviet consumer. Now, almost before being ousted, Khrushchev had to confirm again his good intentions of increasing the production of such goods as refrigerators, washing machines, vacuum cleaners, and electrical appliances. The output was promised to be increased fourfold over the year 1963, but the promise came shortly before Khrushchev departed from office and thus he was never given the chance to carry out the oft repeated promise to satisfy the "material and spiritual needs" of the patient consumers.

History will be more objective in judging Premier Khrushchev's record of achievements. In one sense it can be said that he came to the footlights of Soviet politics as a transitional leader; he came to power after a quarter of a century of Stalin's rule which, he realized, needed a drastic overhaul. It is amazing how far he succeeded in moving ahead. He sensed acutely the need of change in industrial management and in the planning system. This, he understood correctly, was the absolute requirement of an economy that had developed into a complex and sophisticated system in a country that only recently witnessed profound social changes: from a rural society the country was rapidly transformed into a modern urban community. With the zeal of a newcomer Khrushchev never hesitated to try policies, drop them, undertake corrective reforms, abandon them when unsatisfactory, and try something else. Managerial reforms succeeded one another in rapid succession, putting emphasis at one stage on local initiative and changing again by returning to centralized control. In agriculture, where he claimed to be particularly experienced, he sought magic solutions such as planting more corn or forming shock brigades for the development of "virgin lands." But all these efforts failed in the end to prevent a disastrous harvest. The price for such failures was natural and in Soviet terms charitable: he was retired, pensioned, and given an apartment near Moscow to spend the rest of his years in complete obscurity.

Economic Changes after Khrushchev. The fall of Khrushchev was bound to bring changes in economic organization as well as new means to improve the balance in Soviet industrial investment policy. During Khrushchev's last year he made many significant administrative alterations which his opponents considered harmful and which in the end caused his downfall. In 1962, for instance, he divided the Communist Party structure into urban and rural hierarchies: one presumably was to concern itself with industry and the other with agriculture. This was repealed shortly after the new leaders, A. N. Kosygin and L. Brezhnev, assumed power. The reason for repealing it, according to the official version of the *Izvestiia* editorial, was because the act originally had been carried out with characteristic unwarranted haste and with no thought whatever as to the consequences. The division was to contribute to increased incompetence, inefficiency, and to shortages of many commodities, asserted the Soviet press.

From the start it was equally clear that the successors

of Khrushchev were determined to undo some of the decisions of recent years initiated by the man of "great and sudden enthusiasms." On the other hand, certain measures were adopted which indicated a firmer pursuit of former lenient policies. The new leaders were determined to make production more responsive to market demands and not to central planning. Along with this the government initiated a drive to rid itself of the accumulated mass of merchandise it was unable to sell for the last few years. Prices were reduced on many articles as much as 50 percent or more. Simultaneously it set out to apply the long-pressed Liberman ideas on a much broader scale.

In January 1965 the Council of National Economy officially ordered some 400 consumer-goods factories to be converted to the Liberman system. The order was to go into effect in several stages beginning April 1, to be applied gradually to all branches of the economy. Thus the system urged by Liberman, which was only cautiously experimented with by Khrushchev was now officially embraced by the government. It was soon announced that the heavy industry of the western Ukraine, including the coal-mining industry, was to start the new system on an experimental basis of demand and supply. The demand-based production system was soon extended to the footwear and garment factories. The government also promised other changes which would favor consumer-oriented goals.

Once the profit motive became the basis for Soviet planning and production the next logical step was the reorganization of the price-control system. Formerly price control was in the hands of a minor Bureau of Prices within the State Planning Committee. The old practice in the Soviet economy was to use prices as a means of planned goals. Now it became necessary, in attaining economic goals, to allow sufficient flexibility to stimulate efficient production. The new self-regulating factor made the old system obsolete. Recent Soviet changes came to resemble the Western economy, where prices were determined by such factors as production, allocation of resources, and consumption. Accordingly, at the end of August 1965 the Soviet government announced the establishment of a new high-level agency as part of the general economic reform based on the profit motive. The head of the new agency, the State Planning Committee, was given ministerial rank and charged with the authority to administer prices.

Another step taken by the government was the announced intention of applying an interest charge on capital, a measure that had been long opposed by orthodox Marxists. The labor theory of value as taught by Marxists regarded such a policy as completely false. Premier Kosygin was also in favor of abandoning the former Marxist belief that production was only for use and not for profit. The Soviet government recently began to emphasize profit as one acceptable criterion of economic efficiency.

In the middle of April 1965 appeared the first clear blueprint of the post-Khrushchev government, outlining the next Five Year Plan. The plan was business-like, free of Khrushchevian glib talk about "burying" capitalism or overtaking the American standard of living. Kosygin repeatedly touched upon the rapidly improved living standards and the wage policy upon which there had been a virtual freeze on increases since 1960. Khrushchev opposed wage increases on the ground that in a Communist society a range of virtually free services like education, medical care, housing, and transportation, rather than money wages, determined living standards. This Kosygin evidently could not agree with. He stated: "We are often still prisoners of canons that we worked out ourselves and that should have beeen replaced long ago by new principles corresponding to present-day conditions. . . . Wages must be placed in direct relationship to increases in labor productivity." It was announced that a minimum wage of 40 to 45 rubles a month had gone into effect January 1, 1965, in industries where it had not been introduced formerly.

The prime concern of the government during the forthcoming years, Kosygin explained further, must be the welfare of the people and the supply of the market with more goods of daily use. He also promised to see that real incomes would rise by 7.3 percent compared with 3.9 percent in 1964, and he aimed at a sustained, balanced growth of the entire economy instead of sporadic shifts in priorities as practiced by the preceding administration. The five year plan which would begin in 1966, Kosygin promised, would provide for a growth of rate of consumer-goods production which would surpass the heavy industry rate.

The recent priorities given to the chemical industry were now altered. The new administration was compelled to scale down the rate of chemical expansion as designated by the ambitious seven year development plan adopted in December 1963, and the saved funds were to be channeled to other needs. By reducing Khrushchev's ambitious chemical program the new government apparently achieved a more balanced economy.

There was only a 13 percent increase during 1964-65 instead of 36 percent as initially planned. Instead of 2.757 billion rubles as originally designated for chemical investment, the new administration cut the chemical outlay to 2.255 billion rubles. The output of chemical fibers had been reduced from 440,000 metric tons in 1965 to 416,000, while production of fertilizers was reduced from 35 million tons to 33.5. On the other hand housing construction was planned for the next five year period to accommodate about 8 million people.

On October 1, 1965, the Soviet government submitted to the Supreme Soviet a bill requesting a recentralization of the nation's industry. The bill, already approved by the Central Committee, provided for the establishment of central industrial ministries, replacing the system of regional management bodies set up by Khrushchev in 1957. Arguing before the Supreme Soviet, Kosygin criticized the existing regional setup and called it cumbersome and inefficient. The recentralization and guidance from central industrial ministries would assure greater economic efficiency. Kosygin added significantly that the new ministerial system did not mean a return to the managerial structure that existed under Stalin.

Defending the bill government spokesmen explained that factory managers must be given greater freedom for initiative. This would reduce interference emanating from petty officials and allow government agencies to manage plants with greater responsibility. The newly established ministries would have an overall supervisory power over their respective industries and authority in planning production, control quality, and carry out coordinated research.

The bill provided for the establishment of 28 ministries. These included 20 ministries that would replace the system of regional industrial councils, and eight ministries that would be converted from "state committees." The latter were established shortly before the fall of Khrushchev. The ministerial system as suggested by the October bill provided for three types of ministries, representing the federal structure of the Soviet Union and its 15 constituent republics. The national ministries directly controlling industrial plants were to be in charge of 9 specialized branches of machinery manufacture, formerly under regional control, and for the natural gas industry and railroad construction, formerly administered by state committees. The Supreme Soviet approved the bill, marking a further departure from Khrushchev's great scheme of industrial decentralization.

Speaking before the meeting of the Central Executive Committee, Leonid Brezhnev openly admitted that the farm program of recent years had come to a dismal failure. Khrushchev calculated that agricultural production during the years 1959-1964 would rise more rapidly than population. This would afford the Soviet people a much improved diet and more abundant merchandise on the national market. In fact what happened was an output increase that at best had barely kept pace with population growth and no surplus for the expected improvements.

The high delivery quotas demanded from the farmers often had the effect of depriving farms of part of their seed stocks, so that the government had to return collected grain to producers. In 1964-1965, Brezhnev said, two million tons of seed had to be returned to farms by the government. Among other farm-aid measures Brezhnev listed an attempt to lower prices of food and manufactured goods, and reduced electric power rates in rural areas and expanded farm electrification, because, of the 40,000 collective farms 12 percent still had no electricity at all. The new leaders disapproved the late practice of converting collective farms into state farms. This policy, favored by Khrushchev, resulted in such gigantic units that they became unmanageable. Said Brezhnev, "at the present stage, our duty is not to accelerate the transformation of one form into another, but to contribute in every way toward the development and prosperity of both types of social economy." The collective farms were promised a reduction in income tax by applying tax rates to net rather than gross income as in former years.

Brezhnev came to realize as did Kosygin that the root of the difficulties was deeply hidden in the collective-farm system. This was best shown by his readiness to encourage small-scale private farming activity and raise prices paid to farmers. Where the money was to come from to pay higher prices and increase projected investment was not clear, but obviously it had to come from other areas of the already overstrained economy. The extra expense, Brezhnev promised, would be absorbed by the government without entailing a rise in retail prices of meat, bread, or milk.

Two policies in particular were involved in the new program which could be regarded as most significant. One included increased incentives for farmers to produce more by reducing their taxes and by raising the prices of their produce. This was bound to add several billion rubles to the income of the collective farmers. The second policy was to make a huge investment in a five year program, about 700 billion rubles during 1966-1970, in order to equip Soviet farmers with up-to-date machinery and extensive irrigation canals. The new administration for the first time placed agriculture on the priority list. Cultivation of corn and the virgin land development were either cancelled or considerably reduced.

Agricultural Reforms. At the end of March 1965 the Soviet government announced some sweeping agricultural reforms. These marked a major shift in the attitude of the government toward the peasantry, long treated as second-class citizens. In the first place, the agriculture wage structure was changed to pay farmers for actual production rather than for work performed. The new program also provided for more investment in agriculture, higher farm prices, lower prices paid by farmers for consumer goods, and lower rural taxes. These reforms were expected to raise the farmers' purchasing power and help reduce the sharp differences in living standards between town and countryside. The proposed reforms emphasized the departure from Khrushchev's farm technique of dictation from above by applying instead economic levers of prices and costs.

The new system was to be tested in selected collective and state farms during 1965 before it was to be applied throughout the country. The wage reform had one aim in mind—to stimulate the lagging output of crops and animal products and help reduce persistently high productive costs. The reform would also have the effect of providing greater stability in the incomes of collective farmers, who are now subject to substantial year-to-year variations.

Under the existing practice, the collective farmer's income was not based on volume of output but on the number of so-called work days put in during the year and the particular skill employed. On state farms, which are owned and operated by the government, workers are paid fixed salaries, as in industry, with wage levels depending on the character of the work. The new payment plan for collective farms provided for a fixed minimum-wage fund. The wage fund must contain at least 25 percent of the farm's money income based on the average of the previous two to five years, and 50 percent of advances paid to the farm by government purchasing agencies for the season's crop deliveries. During the year, collective farmers will receive guaranteed monthly advance payment totalling 60 to 80 percent of their annual incomes.

In the final year-end accounting, farmers would receive the remainder, including a fixed rate for each quart of milk or bushel of wheat produced. They would also receive bonuses for reducing costs, raising quality, and maintaining production schedules. The present system of paying at least part of the collective farmers' year-end balance in kind would be retained.

On the state farms, the output of workers would also be the basic criterion for determining their incomes. Pay rates would vary for each crop and for each type of animal product. In a parallel development, Soviet authorities were working on a new system of prices paid to collective and state farms for produce. The new prices were intended to reduce the gap between poor farms, working under adverse climatic and other natural conditions, and rich farms that benefit from fertile soil and favorable climate. Both plans suggested that the new Soviet leadership was coping with farm problems in a quiet manner and with the counsel of academic economists, in contrast to former widely publicized schemes by Khrushchev that often ignored scientific recommendations.

Among the many changes, the heart of the reforms was the decision to more than double the investment in agriculture in the five year plan of 1966-1970 as compared with that of the last five years. Brezhnev announced at the plenary meeting of the party's Central Committee in March 1965 that the total investment from the government budget and from the funds of the collective and state farms would be 71 billion rubles. The comparable figure for 1960-1964 was approximately 33 billion rubles. He added that compulsory grain collections would be reduced in 1965 from 65.5 million tons to 55.7 million and that the new annual level would be maintained until 1970. This meant not only that a greater share of grain would be retained by the farms for their own needs but also that they would be able to plan crops over a longer range instead of having to depend on annual changes in government procurement plans.

Industrial Gains. By April 1965 the Soviet government was able to report that the decline of the industrial production growth rate in the last two years had been checked. The official first-quarter report on the performance of industry indicated that the country was on the road to recovery from the catastrophic crop failure of 1963. The economic report listed record production of meat and butter in government slaughterhouses and dairies.

According to the announcement, total industrial output in the first three months of 1965 was 9 percent higher than production in the corresponding period of the previous year. The decline in industrial growth which had been evident since 1962 reached the low point of 7.1 percent for all of the year 1964. The latest economic report showed steady rates for the key industrial commodities of heavy industry and consumer durables, television sets, washing machines, radios, and others. Most marked advances, however, were evident in the recovery of the food industry from the poor 1963 crop. Butter production was at a record high of 142,000 tons compared with 88,000 tons last year. State meat output recovered similarly from 776,000 tons in the first quarter of 1964 to 893,000 in the first quarter of 1965.

Soviet Asian Developments. For some time there had been a wide gap between the energy-deficient though highly industrialized part of the Soviet Union in the west and the energy abundant underdeveloped part in Soviet Siberia and Central Asia. Upon the proper transfer of electric power to European parts of the Soviet Union rests the key of development; future industrial expansion will depend upon successful exploitation of the potential power sources of the east. The European part of the Soviet Union contains most of the population and most of the manufacturing capacity, yet it contains only 20 percent of the nation's total fuel and hydroelectric resources. On the other hand, the less-populated eastern regions contain some of the richest deposits of coal, oil, and gas, and swift flowing streams with enormous generating potential.

In June 1965 the government announced plans for construction of a huge power-generating center in Central Asia to feed European Russia; the construction is to consist of three or four generating plants. Each plant is to have a capacity of 3.8 million kilowatts with super-high tension transmission lines that will cover a distance of 1,500 miles into western Russia. The planned 1.5 million-volt direct-current line would be the first major link between Soviet Asia and the European section. Construction of the stations is to be completed within six to eight years. The entire complex will also supply the industries of the Ural region through a 750,000-volt branch line about 650 miles long.

A new industrial center has been rising in the heart of Siberia around the city of Bratsk (see page 73) with a population of about 35,000 and several scattered settlements in the nearby forest areas. The total population

is about 140,000. Living conditions are harsh and workers here draw an average wage of about 165 to 200
dollars a month plus 40 percent premium for work under
far northern conditions. This is approximately twice the
monthly earnings of the worker in the European part of
the Soviet Union.

The Bratsk timber processing complex under construction since 1960 was designed to turn 250,000 cubic feet
of logs into woodpulp, cardboard for boxes, newsprint,
plywood, and a host of chemical wood products. The
determining factors in locating the mill at Bratsk were
the immense forest resources of Siberia, the unusually
clean water carried by the Angara River out of Lake
Baikal, and the availability of an experienced, well-
equipped construction force that was made idle after the
completion of the Bratsk power project.

The Bratsk mill will produce pulp for the making of
tire cord at a tire-manufacturing complex planned at
Saratov on the Volga River. The mill's output of box-
board reflects the profound changes under way in the
Soviet packaging industry, where wood has been traditional material for making boxes and crates. Half the
mill's capacity was scheduled to go into operation in
1966, and the rest by 1970 on the shore of the reservoir
formed by the world's largest hydroelectric station. The
timber-processing complex is one of the two major industries developing at Bratsk. A second enterprise, an
aluminum plant that is to be one of the world's largest
with a capacity of 700,000 tons, is under construction at
the western suburb of Anzeba. (*See Reading No. 34.*)

The Outlook in 1965. The economic report of July
1965 held out some further encouraging notes, though
not in all fields. There were promising signs of greatly
increased farm production. The increased flow of grain,
meat, and vegetables contributed to a similar rise in production in meat processing plants, in the clothing and
shoe factories, the textile raw materials and leather. But
there was a dimmer side of the picture after the 1965
harvest. The farmers worked harder, were paid higher
prices for their produce, and earned a higher annual income. Still by the middle of August it became clear that
the 1965 harvest and the consequent Soviet purchases of

wheat from the West during the same month signaled an inauspicious beginning for the ambitious agricultural plans of the post-Khrushchev leaders. At this time of the season it already became an open secret that the 1965 harvest was not a disastrous one as in 1963, nevertheless it was far below the level needed to launch the course announced by Brezhnev in March. Early in September 1965 the government had begun to finance massive imports of grain for the second time in three years. A first sale of 100 tons of gold was made to the Bank for International Settlements in Basel, for resale to the central banker's Gold Pool. This amounts to $112,525,000 at $35.00 an ounce, or half of what the Soviet government needs to pay for the wheat it intended to import from Canada in 1965. The Soviet government planned to import as much as nine million tons of grain from Canada, Argentina, Australia, and France by the end of 1965.

The Soviet Union had made great advances in industrialization and technology, but it had failed to match the revolution that had taken place in American agriculture. Already before the final figures for the 1965 harvest were available qualified sources estimated the gross wheat crop about 60 million tons. The 1964 harvest yielded 74.2 million tons of wheat, while the disastrous year of 1963 produced 49.7 million tons. Anticipating shortages the Soviet government hastened to purchase during the August weeks six million tons of wheat from Canada and Argentine at the cost of about 530 million dollars. Because United States wheat was too costly Canada and Argentine had received windfalls. The reason for U.S. wheat being more costly was that the American government required that at least 50 percent of wheat exports to Soviet-bloc countries must be shipped in American vessels. By this requirement the United States excluded itself from what would have otherwise proven a profitable deal—it would have improved Soviet-American relations and helped the sale of the nation's surplus wheat.

The result of the crop failure was that the Soviet Union had its greatest recorded postwar deficit in its trade with Western countries. The deficit affected the Soviet foreign trade balance as a whole, resulting in an

excess of imports over exports. This is particularly noteworthy since the Soviet Union's international trade balance has been favorable in most years since 1955. According to 1964 trade statistics, the imbalance in trade
with the West resulted largely from emergency purchases of wheat. The Soviet government had to dip into
its gold reserves to pay for imported grain. The irony of
the situation was that wheat was bought mainly from
Canada, Australia, and the United States, three countries
whose imports from the Soviet Union are negligible.

Total Soviet imports from Western nations in 1964
were $1.776 billion and exports to the same countries
$1.332 billion, a deficit of $444 million. The total deficit
in Soviet trade was $55.5 million. Needless to say, the
spending of valuable currency on wheat imports was
bound to inhibit Soviet investment in consumer industries and other branches of the economy. It was equally
bound to have a negative effect on diplomatic relations
with the underdeveloped countries that were expecting
to receive Soviet aid. The economic difficulties, as during
the previous years and similar experiences, were caused
by adverse weather conditions: a dry June when rain is
needed and a wet July and August when dry weather
for harvesting is important. Now the post-Khrushchev
leaders were forced to carry out the program they envisioned in more difficult conditions.

The July 1965 report held out greater promise in industry than did the report of the first half of the previous
year. The declining trend in the growth rate of Soviet
industrial production had now been reversed. The Soviet
Union's economy rose 9.3 per cent in the first six months
over the 1964 period. Labor productivity in industry was
5.4 per cent higher and industrial production cost had
been lowered according to plan. The population of the
Soviet Union on July 1, 1965 rose to 230.5 million.

The report proved particularly impressive where it indicated a better-than-average improvement in consumer
goods production. Housewives were able to buy more for
their rubles than they could a year ago. The report indicated that price cuts on cloth and garments in April
represented an annual gain of 1.1 billion rubles to consumers. At the same time prices in the food market were

down 17 per cent by comparison with the first half of last year. The general sentiment by the fall of 1965 was that the new team of Brezhnev-Kosygin had been coping with the economic difficulties more successfully than their predecessor, Nikita S. Khrushchev.

Finally, it should be noted, Libermanism had taken deeper roots in 1965. In September 1965 the 174 member Central Committee of the Communist Party met and endorsed sweeping reforms intended to make the national industry more efficient. Soviet factories henceforth were to face keener competition from each other while prices and profits had to become key factors in the economy. The 12-men presidium delivered a report "on improving the management of industry, perfecting planning and strengthening the economic incentives of industrial production." The report not only called for a new system of incentives based on goods sold rather than goods produced, but also on whittling down of bureaucracy.

Loosening Government Controls. The September meeting of the Central Committee devoted much attention to the loosening of centralized controls. This called for a carefully planned transition that would lead to a weakening of controls over government-owned industrial enterprises. Factory managers were assigned greater initiative; prices, costs, and market relationships, formerly associated only with capitalist economics, were now more carefully considered. The reform adopted by the committee can be considered as one of the three turning points in the economic history of the USSR. The first one was the New Economic Policy initiated in 1921; the second one the rigidly planned economy intended to industrialize the country, inaugurated in 1928; the third stage in 1965, when the former rigid economy was to yield to a mixed system of central planning aided by greater managerial initiative.

The enforcement of the new program implied great risks and called for much perseverance. To begin with, the government selected some fifty plants in various parts of the Soviet Union. These were to represent a broad range of industries. In the Moscow region some twenty enterprises have already been chosen as experimental units. To these were added later such widely scattered plants as the Norilsk nonferrous-metals smelter in northern Siberia, the steel plant of Volgograd, and food processing, chemical and construction materials, and other industries.

The central government agencies were to assume a minimum assignment in planning, mostly counselling on overall goals. The chosen plants had to assume greater responsibility and their performance would be judged not by their gross output in monetary terms, but their ability to sell the specific assortments of goods ordered by customers. This led to an awareness of the principle that goods must be sold to be paid for. It meant that an effective market had to influence production. Such a market had to force each enterprise to produce not only up-to-date patterns within its capability, but turn out most wanted commodities. An increased share of profits was to be channeled into the government treasury or placed at the disposal of the factories for small investment, bonuses, and other worker benefits.

There was another important novelty added in the newly adopted policy. Large-scale investment for plant expansion or construction of new enterprises was now to be financed by interest-bearing loans instead of outright budgetary grants as in the past. To secure efficient use of investments on plant and equipment, formerly squandered by being supplied free of charge to industrial managers, enterprises were expected to pay a fixed return out of their profits into the government treasury, based on the total value of their fixed assets. And whereas prices were formerly arbitrarily set so that a factory operating with normal efficiency would make a profit, under the new system wholesale prices were to be based on actual production cost. The five year plan to be launched in 1966 expected gradually to make the transition and convert the entire national industry to the new system.

Economic Gains in 1965. The recently published report of the Central Statistical Board (*See Reading No. 34*) revealed impressive gains as well as serious failures in national income, in agricultural output, and in housing and wages that were targeted in the overambitious seven-year plan. Wage figures, traditionally secret, were based on economic results of the past year. The report revealed that the nation's 77 million nonagricultural workers earned a monthly average of $105.55 (99 rubles). This was up $5.55 from 1964 and was exactly double the 1946 figure. If one were to add such fringe benefits as bonuses or free medical care, the real average income of factory, office, and commercial workers was $142.22 (128 rubles) a month in 1965. According to the same report the total output of the Soviet Union in 1965 had risen almost 7 percent—the highest of any major nation in the world—compared with 7 percent in 1964 and with the postwar low of 4 percent in 1963. (Measured by United States standards, the State Department estimated that the Soviet growth rate averaged only 4.3 percent during 1960-1965. Soviet figures for the same six year period show an average gain of 6.4 percent for the Soviet economy. The discrepancy is largely due to the different statistical measurement used by the two governments.)

According to the same report production of consumer goods in 1965 is listed as 8.5 percent above 1964, whereas in 1963 the gain had been 3 percent over 1962, and in 1964 the increase over 1963 was 5.1 percent. Production of refrigerators and washing machines, two of the most closely watched items of consumer production, had risen to as much as 48 and 20 percent respectively from 1964 to 1965. On the other hand, housing construction, a continually weak point, failed to meet the 1965 target despite an increase over 1964. The major failure admitted in the report was in grain production. Drought caused a drop from 162.1 million metric tons in 1964 to 120.5 million in 1965. The serious grain failure, the report implies, was bound to result in a drop in the growth rate on consumer goods from 8.5 percent in 1965 to 6.0 percent in 1966.

Agriculture, 1965. The key problem in the Soviet economy by the end of 1965 remained agriculture. Early in 1966 the Communist Party named Leonid I. Brezhnev, its First Secretary, chairman of a commission to draft a new collective-farm charter that might improve the situation. The commission consisted of 149 members, including top party members, farm scientists, chairmen of collective farms, regular farmers, and agricultural officials. The purpose of this commission was to adopt new statutes listing rights and obligations of some 37,000 collective farms and their members. The present farm charter was made obsolete by the many mergers that had increased the size of the average farm fivefold. It was outdated further by the transfer of farm machinery from 58 government Machine Tractor Stations to the ownership of collective farms themselves, and by changes in payment practices.

Agriculture, 1966. By the end of August 1966 encouragement came from the fact that the 1966 wheat harvest of the USSR has been virtually completed and might possibly approach the bumper harvest of 1964. It has been estimated that the 1966 crop would exceed 70 million tons, which was 10 million tons more than the crop of 1965, though is short of the 1964 harvest of 74.2 million tons. Combined with the 3 million tons of wheat purchased from Canada and 800,000 tons from France, it was very likely that the USSR would be adequately equipped and even manage to build some reserves.

The purchase of wheat from abroad was contracted for 3 years in advance thereby assuring the Soviet Union against future economic fluctuations or political complications. The 1966 outlook is such that the Soviet Union might even manage without grain importation. Experts estimated the total annual need of the country of approximately 70 million tons, including the aid Moscow must extend to other communist countries in Eastern Europe. This would permit the Soviet government a modest replenishment of its badly depleted reserves.

Industry, 1966. Appearing before the Supreme Soviet early in August 1966, Premier Kosygin reported on the next five-year economic development plan as approved in April by the 23rd Congress of the Soviet Communist Party. After the Congress approved the plan and details were worked out, it was to be submitted to the Supreme Soviet to be enacted into law. But Premier Kosygin had to explain that the plan was delayed until some minor difficulties were ironed out. The disputes over prices and management caused mainly the delay. Wholesale prices are usually fixed in the USSR by a government committee which on many occasions failed to take into consideration actual cost of materials and production. The government now sought a settlement of this problem before the final adoption of the plan, hence the delay. Officials still hesitated to allow price fluctuation in accordance with supply and demand.

Explaining further the goals of the plan Premier Kosygin added that it aimed to insure the growth of national income by 38-41 percent, increase the volume of industrial production about 50 percent and the average volume of agricultural output by 25 percent as against the previous five-year period. Furthermore, living standards must be raised by increasing real per capita income by approximately 30 percent and close the gap between the levels and living conditions of town and village working people. Finally, that the plan would continue to place emphasis on consumer goods.

Foreign Aid Reduced. Domestic problems were bound to affect foreign policy. The most noticeable impact was the projected cut in the Soviet foreign aid program. Foreign aid began in 1954, providing long-term, low-interest credits to Communist states and grants to non-Communist underdeveloped countries. It has been reported that the biggest Soviet aid beneficiary, India, had been informed as early as 1965 that due to domestic economic pressure the aid program would have to be restricted. A similar policy has been followed in regard to other countries. Kenya had to turn down Soviet aid because it was tied to the sale of Soviet goods in that country. Since 1954 the Soviet Union provided about 10 billion dollars worth of aid to both Communist and underdeveloped countries. Long-term, low-interest credits, amounting to about 3.9 billion dollars, had been extended to 28 nations. Western figures on Soviet aid show 4.268 billion dollars worth of credit and grant commitments through 1964, though only 1.5 billion dollars actually had been spent.

That cuts in Soviet foreign aid will be carried out is generally accepted, though it is believed that a complete stoppage is hardly possible. Soviet investment is too heavy for it to abandon entirely such major aid receivers as India, the United Arab Republic, Indonesia, Afghanistan, or Algeria. These five recipients alone account for three quarters of total Soviet commitments. India had been promised 1.022 billion dollars in aid through 1964, the United Arab Republic 899 million dollars, Afghanistan 541 million dollars, Indonesia 369 million dollars, and Algeria 229 million dollars. This aid is mostly in industrial goods tied to specifically chosen projects.

The Eighth Five Year Plan, 1966-1970. Early in 1966 the Soviet government announced the blueprints of the new economic plan. The latest plan promised to give Soviet citizens a better material life by 1970. It based the plan for economic advancement on an enduring peace. While announcing the economic targets of the plan the official press significantly added that defense capacity must be maintained even though "the most vital task is not to allow a new world war to break out." The latest plan acknowledged that certain long-range production goals set in 1961 have not been fulfilled mainly because these were initially overoptimistic. The Eighth Five Year Plan had realigned priorities, given greater emphasis to consumer goods and agricultural production, promised higher earnings, more passenger cars, and more and better food products.

This plan was based on the assumption of a durable peace during which the nation would derive utmost benefits from increased prosperity. It envisaged an increase in the national income from 38 to 41 percent, a rise in industrial output of some 50 percent and in per capita incomes about 30 percent. The planners hoped by special measures to narrow the gap in living standards between urban and rural dwellers. The plan called for some 50 percent increase in production of capital goods and about 45 percent increase in consumer goods. The most promising benefit to Soviet consumers was the promise of a sharply increased production of automobiles. Passenger car production by 1970 was to be four times greater than in 1965, from 616,400 to 1.5 million. Foreign experts considered the 1966 plan more realistic than the exuberantly optimistic plan of 1959.

A realistic appraisal of the latest plan does not permit the nation to hope that by 1970 all consumer needs will be satisfied. It is true that when one compares the economic growth rates of the preceding five year plan with the planned rates for the succeeding plan of 1966-1970, there is an obvious effort to bring a speedup. Thus the national income in 1961-1965 rose only 6 percent annually while the 1966-1970 plan provided for a 6.7-7.1 percent increase. Agriculture, which had done most poorly and grew only 2 percent, is projected for a 5.63 percent growth. By 1970 the grain production rate calls for 169.5 million tons a year. This is about the same amount former Premier Khrushchev promised in 1959 to achieve by 1965. But weather conditions, as we have seen, caused a drop to 120.5 million. As on previous occasions, weather still remained a factor not to be minimized, or, in the words of one Soviet economist, much must depend on "the one above."

Though national defense remained vital, in the latest plan heavy industry was getting a reduced priority. The growth of heavy industry from 1966 to 1970 was set at 49-52 percent while consumer goods production at 43-46 percent. There is abundant evidence that the key motive of recent developments in the Soviet Union was the conversion of the country into a consumer-oriented economy, though the prospects of affluence still remain distant. The official admission is that by 1970 the Soviet consumer will enjoy more goods, but he will by no means be able to satisfy fully all consumption demands.

It is premature to guess whether the preservation of centralized controls, the continued top-heavy national investments in arms, in the space program and in capital goods, and the promise to add an increased emphasis to production of consumer goods will prove a successful undertaking. The none too robust Soviet economy cannot bear for too long the burden of high space expenditures without impairing gravely the good intentions to supply the hungry consumer. It is idle to try to guess whether the new leaders will precede or follow shifts in policy. It is equally idle to venture predictions of world developments upon which Soviet policies must depend, involving the success or failure of the economic plan. Meanwhile one thing is certain: the world will watch with

keen interest whether the embarkation upon the enlarge-
ment of independence of industrial units (Libermanism)
and the demand for economic stimuli within the framework of Marxist national ownership of means of production will enable the Soviet Union to compete successfully with the free-enterprise Western capitalist system.

Part II

READINGS

— Reading No. 1 —

SOCIAL INSURANCE*

Decree of the Sovnarkom, November 13, 1917

The Workers' and Peasants' Government, being supported by the Soviet of Workers', Soldiers', and Peasants', announces to the working class of Russia and to the city and village poor that it will immediately prepare decrees on social insurance in accordance with the ideas of the workers.

1. Insurance for all wage workers without exception, as well as for the city and village poor.

2. Insurance to cover all forms of disability, such as illness, injury, invalidism, old age, maternity, widowhood, orphanage, as well as unemployment.

3. The total cost of the insurance to be borne by the employer.

4. Full compensation in case of disability or unemployment.

5. The insured to have full control of the insurance institutions.

In the name of the Government of the Russian people.

A. SHLIAPNIKOV
People's Commissar of Labor

* Reprinted from *The Bolshevik Revolution, 1917-1918* by James Bunyan and H. H. Fisher with the permission of the publishers, Stanford University Press. Copyright 1934 by the Board of Trustees of The Leland Stanford Junior University, renewed 1961 by James Bunyan and H. H. Fisher.

NATIONALIZATION OF BANKS*

Decree of the Central Executive Committee,
December 27, 1917

In the interests of a proper organization of the national economy, a thorough eradication of bank speculation and a complete emancipation of the toiling masses from exploitation by the banking capitalists, and in order to found a single unified State Bank for the Russian Republic which shall serve the interests of the people and the poorest classes, the Central Executive Committee decrees that:

1. Banking is hereby declared a state monopoly.

2. All existing private joint-stock banks and other banking houses are to become a part of the State Bank.

3. Assets and liabilities of establishments in the process of liquidation will be assumed by the State Bank.

4. The manner of the amalgamation of private banks with the State Bank will be determined by a special decree.

5. The temporary management of private banks is intrusted to the Council of the State Bank.

6. The interests of small depositors will be fully protected.

SEARCH OF SAFE DEPOSIT BOXES

Decree of the Central Executive Committee,
December 27, 1917

1. All money kept in safe deposit boxes should be transferred to the current account of the holders.

* Reprinted from *The Bolshevik Revolution, 1917-1918* by James Bunyan and H. H. Fisher with the permission of the publishers, Stanford University Press. Copyright 1934 by the Board of Trustees of The Leland Stanford Junior University, renewed 1961 by James Bunyan and H. H. Fisher.

Note: Gold in coin or bullion is to be confiscated and handed over to the State Gold Reserve.

2. All holders of safe deposit boxes are under obligation to appear at the bank upon notice, bringing the keys to their safe deposit boxes, and to be present while their boxes are searched.

3. All holders of safe deposit boxes who fail to appear after three days' notice will be considered as having maliciously declined to comply with the law of search.

4. Safe deposit boxes owned by persons who maliciously decline to comply with the law will be opened by investigating commissions appointed by the Commissar of the State Bank; all property contained in those vaults will be confiscated and declared the property of the people.

— Reading No. 3 —

REGULATION FOR THE CONFISCATION OF INDUSTRIAL ENTERPRISES*

Resolution of the Supreme Council of National Economy, February 16, 1918

1. The confiscation of industrial and other enterprises is to be conducted according to a well-defined state plan of economy by: (a) the Supreme Council of National Economy, and (b) the Soviet of People's Commissars.

2. From now on no institution other than those indi-

* Reprinted from *The Bolshevik Revolution, 1917-1918* by James Bunyan and H. H. Fisher with the permission of the publishers, Stanford University Press. Copyright 1934 by the Board of Trustees of The Leland Stanford Junior University, renewed 1961 by James Bunyan and H. H. Fisher.

cated in Article 1 has a right to confiscate enterprises. Institutions that have already made confiscations should report all these to the Supreme Council of National Economy.

3. Proposals to the Soviet of People's Commissars from any department, institution, or person, suggesting that some enterprise be confiscated, must be accompanied by a statement of the Supreme Council of National Economy.

4. All questions concerning the confiscation of enterprises are to be forwarded to that bureau of the Supreme Council of National Economy which deals with the organization of production, and the decisions of the bureau are to be submitted for approval to the presidium.

— Reading No. 4 —

NATIONALIZATION OF FOREIGN TRADE*

Decree of the Sovnarkom, April 22, 1918

I

All foreign trade is to be nationalized. Contracts with foreign countries and foreign commercial houses for buying and selling all kinds of products (raw, industrial, agricultural, etc.) are to be made in the name of the Russian Republic by specially authorized organs. Aside from these organs all export and import agreements are forbidden.

Note: Regulations for the import and export of packages and travelers' baggage will be published separately.

* Reprinted from *The Bolshevik Revolution, 1917-1918* by James Bunyan and H. H. Fisher with the permission of the publishers, Stanford University Press. Copyright 1934 by the Board of Trustees of The Leland Stanford Junior University, renewed 1961 by James Bunyan and H. H. Fisher.

II

The People's Commissariat of Trade and Industry is the organ in charge of nationalized foreign trade. . . .

VI

The present decree will become effective from the moment of its publication.

V. ULIANOV (LENIN)
President of the Soviet of People's
Commissars
GUKOVSKY, BRONSKY, STALIN, CHICHERIN,
People's Commissars

— Reading No. 5 —

ABOLITION OF INHERITANCE*

Decree of the Central Executive Committee,
April 27, 1918

I. Inheritance by law or testament is hereby abolished. After the death of the owner, his property (personal and real) becomes the property of the Russian Socialist Federated Soviet Republic. . . .

V. All the property of the decedent, except that which is listed in Article IX of this decree [property of decedent which does not exceed 10,000 rubles and consists principally of house and garden, furniture, and implements of a worker's establishment], is taken over by the soviet of the place where the person resided before his death or where the property in question is located. The soviet

* Reprinted from *The Bolshevik Revolution, 1917-1918* by James Bunyan and H. H. Fisher with the permission of the publishers, Stanford University Press. Copyright 1934 by the Board of Trustees of The Leland Stanford Junior University, renewed 1961 by James Bunyan and H. H. Fisher.

turns over this property to the local institutions in charge
of the various properties belonging to the Russian Republic. . . .

> YA. SVERDLOV
> Chairman of the All-Russian
> Central Executive Committee

— Reading No. 6 —

NATIONALIZATION OF LARGE-SCALE INDUSTRY*

Decree of the Sovnarkom, June 28, 1918

For the purpose of combating decisively the economic
disorganization and the breakdown of the food supply,
and establishing more firmly the dictatorship of the working class and the village poor, the Soviet of People's
Commissars has resolved:

I. To declare all of the following industrial and commercial enterprises which are located in the Soviet Republic, with all their capital and property, whatever they
may consist of, the property of the Russian Socialist
Federated Soviet Republic. . . .

[A list of mines, mills, factories, etc., follows.]

II. The administration of the nationalized industries
shall be organized . . . by the different departments of
the Supreme Council of National Economy. . . . All
previous decrees issued on the subject of nationalization
remain in force. . . .

V. The entire personnel of every enterprise—tech-

---

* From: James Bunyan. *Intervention, Civil War, and Communism in Russia.* Baltimore, The Johns Hopkins Press,
1936. Pages 397-99.

nicians, workers, members of the board of directors, and foremen—shall be considered employees of the Russian Socialist Federated Soviet Republic; their wages shall be fixed in accordance with the scales existing at the time of nationalization and shall be paid out of the funds of the respective enterprises. Those who leave their posts . . . are liable to the Revolutionary Tribunal and to the full penalty of the law.

VI. All private capital belonging to members of the boards of directors, stockholders, and owners of the nationalized enterprises will be attached pending the determination of the relation of such capital to the turnover capital and resources of the enterprises in question. . . .

X. The present decree becomes effective on the day it is signed.

> V. ULIANOV (LENIN)
> President of the Soviet of
> People's Commissars
> TSIURUPA, NOGIN, RYKOV
> People's Commissars

— Reading No. 7 —

ABOLITION OF THE OWNERSHIP OF REAL ESTATE*

Decree of the Central Executive Committee,
August 20, 1918

1. The right to own a tract of land . . . within a city is abolished without exception.

* From: James Bunyan. *Intervention, Civil War, and Communism in Russia.* Baltimore, The Johns Hopkins Press, 1936. Pages 426-27.

2. The right to own buildings located in cities with a population of 10,000 or over and having . . . a value . . . in excess of the amount fixed by local authorities is abolished. . . .

9. All mortgages of 10,000 rubles or over on confiscated lands and buildings are annulled. Mortgages of less than ten thousand rubles become state loans subject to regulations of the decree annulling state loans.

YA. SVERDLOV
Chairman of the Central
Executive Committee

— Reading No. 8 —

CONSTITUTION (FUNDAMENTAL LAW) OF THE RUSSIAN SOCIALIST FEDERATED SOVIET REPUBLIC*

Adopted by the Fifth All-Russian Congress
of Soviets, July 10, 1918

CHAPTER TWO

3. With the fundamental aim of abolishing all exploitation of man by man, of eliminating completely the division of society into classes, of ruthlessly crushing exploiters, or establishing the socialist organization of society, and of bringing about the triumph of socialism in all countries, the Fifth All-Russian Congress of Soviets of Workers', Soldiers', and Peasants' Deputies further decrees:

* From: James Bunyan. *Intervention, Civil War, and Communism in Russia.* Baltimore, The Johns Hopkins Press, 1936. Pages 508-09.

(a) In order to introduce the socialization of land, private ownership of land is abolished and all land is hereby declared the property and is turned over to the toilers without compensation and with equal rights to its use.

(b) All nationally important forests, subsoil resources, and waters, as well as all live stock and farm appurtenances, model farms, and agricultural enterprises, are declared national property.

(c) As a first step toward the complete transfer of factories, shops, mines, railroads, and other means of production and transportation to the Soviet Republic of Workers and Peasants, and in order to insure the supremacy of the toiling masses over the exploiters, the Congress ratifies the Soviet laws establishing Workers' Control and the Supreme Council of National Economy. . . .

(e) The transfer of all banks to the ownership of the Workers' and Peasants' Government is ratified as one of the prerequisites for the emancipation of the toiling masses from the yoke of capital.

— Reading No. 9 —

THE NEW ECONOMIC POLICY*

From Lenin's Speech of March 1921

Lifted up on a wave of exaltation, and having behind us the general political and, later, the military enthusiasm of the people, we intended on the basis of this enthusiasm to carry out . . . similarly exalted economic tasks. We expected—or perhaps it would be more correct to say that we assumed without sufficient calculations—that

* From: V. I. Lenin. *Works,* Vol. XXVII. Page 29.

by the direct fiat of the proletarian state we would be
able to establish state production and state distribution of
products on a communistic basis in a country of small
peasants. Life has exposed our error. There was a need
of a series of transition stages . . . to communism. . . .
Thus spoke life itself to us. Thus spoke the facts revealed
by the revolution. . . . The fundamental question, from
the point of view of strategy, is, Who will take sooner
advantage of this new situation? Who will win? The
capitalist whom we are now letting in through the door
or even through several doors which we ourselves ignore
and which will open independently of us and against us?
Or the sovereign power of the proletariat?

— Reading No. 10 —

COMPARATIVE OUTPUT OF SOME LEADING PRODUCTS, 1913-1928*

Product	1913	1928
Pig-iron, m. tons	4.2	3.3
Steel, m. tons	4.2	4.3
Rolled steel, m. tons	3.6	3.4
Coal, m. tons	29.1	35.5
Oil, m. tons	9.2	11.7
Electricity, md. kwt	2	5
Copper, 1000 tons	—	19.1
Cement, m. tons	1.5	1.8
Railway locomotives	418	478
Tractors, 1000's	—	1.2
Motor vehicles, 1000's	—	0.7
Grain, m. tons	80-82	73
Sugar, 1000 tons	1290	1283
Cotton cloth, m. metres	227	2742
Woolen cloth, m. metres	95	93
Leather footwear, m. pairs	—	29.6

* From: Maurice Dobb. *Soviet Economic Development since 1917*. New York, International Publishers, 1948. Page 311.

BASIC INDICATOR OF THE ECONOMIC DEVELOPMENT OF THE SOVIET UNION PROJECTED UNDER THE FIVE YEAR PLAN*

(in billions of rubles, at 1926-1927 prices)

	1927-28	1932-33	% increase
Total basic capital at end of year	69.8	126.9	82
Capital investments in entire national economy	8.2	27.7	238
National income (net production)	24.4	49.7	103
Basic capital of industry at end of year	9.6	30.7	220
Capital investments in industry	1.9	7.4	290
Gross production of all industry	18.3	43.2	136
Capital investments in transportation	0.95	4.65	389
Construction of buildings & structures	2.6	12.5	381
Producers' prices (1926-27 = 1,000) general index of industrial prices	961.0	731.0	−24
Index of cost of living of the Central Statistical Administration (1913 = 1,000)	2,050.0	1,760.0	−14

* From: American-Russian Chamber of Commerce. *Economic Handbook of the Soviet Union.* New York, 1931. Page 11.

— Reading No. 12 —

GROSS PRODUCTIONS OF CENSUS INDUSTRIES DURING THE PERIOD OF THE FIVE YEAR PLAN*

(*in billions of rubles, at 1926-1927 prices*)

Industries by groups	Planned for 1932-33	1928	1929	1930	1931	1932
All industries	36.6	15.7	19.8	25.2	30.9	34.3
Heavy industry	17.4	7.0	9.0	12.7	16.0	18.0
Light industry	19.2	8.7	10.8	12.5	14.9	16.3
Percentage of heavy industry		44.3	45.5	50.4	51.8	52.5
Percentage of light industry to total		55.7	54.5	49.6	48.2	47.5

* From: Report of the State Planning Commission of the Council of People's Commissars of the USSR. *Summary of the Fulfilment of the First Five Year Plan.* Moscow, 1933. Page 272.

— Reading No. 13 —

LIQUIDATION OF THE KULAKS*

. . . The kulak class, as a class, cannot be squeezed out by taxation measures and all sorts of other restrictions while the means of production are left in the hands of that class and it enjoys the right of freely using the land, while the law which permits the hiring of labor in rural districts, the law which permits the renting of land and the ban of expropriation of the kulaks remain in operation. . . . In order to squeeze out the kulaks as a class we must break down the resistance of this class in open battle and deprive it of the productive sources of its existence. . . . Without this, collectivization, let alone total collectivization of the rural districts, is inconceivable.

— Reading No. 14 —

NO SLOWDOWN IN TEMPO! †

From the Speech Delivered by Stalin Before the First Conference of Industrial Managers, February 4, 1931

It is sometimes asked whether it is not possible to slow down the tempo somewhat, to put a check on the movement. No, comrades, it is not possible! The tempo

* From: Stalin's speech in 1929.
† From: *Pravda*, February 5, 1931.

must not be reduced! On the contrary, we must increase it as much as is within our powers and possibilities. This is dictated to us by our obligations to the workers and peasants of the U.S.S.R. This is dictated to us by our obligations to the working class of the whole world.

To slacken the tempo would mean falling behind. And those who fall behind get beaten. But we do not want to be beaten. No, we refuse to be beaten! One feature of the history of old Russia was the continual beatings she suffered because of her backwardness. She was beaten by the Mongol khans. She was beaten by the Turkish beys. She was beaten by the Swedish feudal lords. She was beaten by the Polish and Lithuanian gentry. She was beaten by the British and French capitalists. She was beaten by the Japanese barons. All beat her—because of her backwardness, cultural backwardness, political backwardness, industrial backwardness, agricultural backwardness. They beat her because to do so was profitable and could be done with impunity. You remember the words of the pre-revolutionary poet: "You are poor and abundant, mighty and impotent, Mother Russia." [From N. A. Nekrasov's "Who Lives Well in Russia?"] Those gentlemen were quite familiar with the verses of the old poet. They beat her, saying: "You are abundant," so one can enrich oneself at your expense. They beat her, saying: "You are poor and impotent," so you can be beaten and plundered with impunity. Such is the law of the exploiters—to beat the backward and the weak. It is the jungle law of capitalism. You are backward, you are weak—therefore you are wrong; hence you can be beaten and enslaved. You are mighty —therefore you are right; hence we must be wary of you.

That is why we must no longer lag behind.

In the past we had no fatherland, nor could we have had one. But now that we have overthrown capitalism and power is in our hands, in the hands of the people, we have a fatherland, and we will uphold its independence. Do you want our socialist fatherland to be beaten and to lose its independence? If you do not want this, you must put an end to its backwardness in the shortest possible time and develop a genuine Bolshevik tempo in building up its socialist economy. There is no other way. That is why Lenin said on the eve of the October Revolution: "Either perish, or overtake and outstrip the advanced capitalist countries."

We are fifty or a hundred years behind the advanced countries. We must make good this distance in ten years. Either we do it, or we shall go under.

That is what our obligations to the workers and peasants of the U.S.S.R. dictate to us.

But we have yet other, more serious and more important, obligations. They are our obligations to the world proletariat. They coincide with our obligations to the workers and peasants of the U.S.S.R. But we place them higher. The working class of the U.S.S.R. is part of the world working class. We achieved victory not solely through the efforts of the working class of the U.S.S.R., but also thanks to the support of the working class of the world. Without this support we would have been torn to pieces long ago. It is said that our country is the shock brigade of the proletariat of all countries. That is well said. But it imposes very serious obligations upon us. Why does the international proletariat support us? How did we merit this support? By the fact that we were the first to hurl ourselves into the battle against capitalism, we were the first to establish working-class state power, we were the first to begin building socialism. By the fact that we are engaged on a cause which, if successful, will transform the whole world and free the entire working class. But what is needed for success? The elimination of our backwardness, the development of a high Boleshevik tempo of construction. We must march forward in such a way that the working class of the whole world, looking at us, may say: There you have my advanced detachment, my shock brigade, my working-class state power, my fatherland; they are engaged on our cause, *our* cause, and they are working well; let us support them against the capitalists and promote the cause of the world revolution. Must we not justify the hopes of the world's working class, must we not fulfill our obligations to them? Yes, we must if we do not want to utterly disgrace ourselves.

Such are our obligations, internal and international.

As you see, they dictate to us a Boleshevik tempo of development.

I will not say that we have accomplished nothing in regard to management of production during these years. In fact, we have accomplished a good deal. We have doubled our industrial output compared with the pre-war level. We have created the largest-scale agricultural production in the world. But we could have accomplished still more if we had tried during this period really to master production, the technique of production, the financial and economic side of it.

In ten years at most we must make good the distance that separates us from the advanced capitalist countries. We have all the "objective" possibilities for this. The only thing lacking is the ability to make proper use of these possibilities. And that depends on us. *Only* on us! It is time we learned to make use of these possibilities. It is time to put an end to the rotten line of one-interference in production. It is time to adopt a new line, one corresponding to the present period—the line of *interfering in everything*. If you are a factory manager—interfere in all the affairs of the factory, look into everything, let nothing escape you, learn and learn again. Bolsheviks must master technique. It is time Bolsheviks themselves became experts. In the period of reconstruction, technique decides everything. And a business executive who does not want to study technique, who does not want to master technique, is a joke and not an executive.

It is said that it is hard to master technique. That is not true! There are no fortresses that Bolsheviks cannot capture. We have solved a number of most difficult problems. We have overthrown capitalism. We have assumed power. We have built up a huge socialist industry. We have transferred the middle peasants on the path of socialism. We have already accomplished what is most important from the point of view of construction. What remains to be done is not so much: to study technique, to master science. And when we have done that we shall develop a tempo of which we dare not even dream at present.

And we shall do it if we really want to.

— Reading No. 15 —

STALIN'S SPEECH DELIVERED AT THE FIRST ALL-UNION CONGRESS OF COLLECTIVE-FARM SHOCK BRIGADES, FEBRUARY 19, 1933*

I
The Collective-Farm Path
Is the Only Right Path

First Question. Is the path which the collective-farm peasantry has taken the right path; is the path of collective farming the right one?

That is not an idle question. You shock brigaders of the collective farms evidently have no doubt that the collective farms are on the right path. Possibly, for that reason, the question will seem superfluous to you. But not all peasants think as you do. There are still not a few among the peasants, even among the collective farmers, who have doubts as to whether the collective-farm path is the right one. And there is nothing surprising about it. . . .

At all events, the new path is not the customary path, is not a beaten path, not yet a fully explored path. Would it not be better to keep to the old path? Would it not be better to wait a little before embarking on the new, collective-farm path? Is it worth while taking the risk?

These are the doubts that are now troubling one section of the laboring peasantry.

Ought we not dispel these doubts? Ought we not to bring these doubts out into the light of day and show what they are worth? Clearly, we ought to.

* From: *Pravda,* February 23, 1933.

Hence, the question I have just put cannot be described as an idle one.

And so, is the path which the collective-farm peasantry has taken the right one?

Some comrades think that the transition to the new path, to the collective-farm path, started in our country three years ago. This is only partly true. Of course, the development of collective farms on a mass scale started in our country three years ago. The transition, as we know, was marked by the routing of the kulaks and by a movement among the vast masses of the poor and middle peasantry to join the collective farms. All that is true. But in order to start this mass transition to the collective farms, certain preliminary conditions had to be available, without which, generally speaking, the mass collective-farm movement would have been inconceivable.

First of all, we had to have the Soviet power, which has helped and continues to help the peasantry to take the collective-farm path.

Secondly, it was necessary to drive out the landlords and the capitalists, to take the factories and the land away from them and declare these the property of the people.

Thirdly, it was necessary to curb the kulaks and to take machines and tractors away from them.

Fourthly, it was necessary to declare that the machines and tractors could be used only by the poor and middle peasants organized in collective farms.

Finally, it was necessary to industrialize the country, to set up a new tractor industry, to build new factories for the manufacture of agricultural machinery, in order to supply tractors and machines in abundance to the collective-farm peasantry.

Without these preliminary conditions there could have been no question of the mass transition to the collective-farm path that started three years ago.

— Reading No. 16 —

DIZZY WITH SUCCESS*

CONCERNING QUESTIONS
OF THE COLLECTIVE-FARM MOVEMENT

The Soviet government's successes in the sphere of the collective-farm movement are now being spoken of by everyone. Even our enemies are forced to admit that the successes are substantial. And they really are very great.

It is a fact that by February 20 of this year 50 per cent of the peasant farms throughout the U.S.S.R. had been collectivized. That means that by February 20, 1930, we had *overfulfilled* the five-year plan of collectivization by more than 100 per cent.

It is a fact that on February 28 of this year the collective farms had *already succeeded* in stocking upwards of 36,000,000 centners, i.e., about 220,000,000 poods, of seed for the spring sowing, which is more than 90 per cent of the plan. It must be admitted that the accumulation of 220,000,000 poods of seed by the collective farms alone—after the successful fulfillment of the grain-procurement plan—is a tremendous achievement.

What does all this show?

That a *radical turn of the countryside towards socialism may be considered as already achieved.*

There is no need to prove that these successes are of supreme importance for the fate of our country, for the whole working class, which is the directing force of our country, and, lastly, for the Party itself. To say nothing of the direct practical results, these successes are of immense value for the internal life of the Party itself, for the education of our Party. They imbue our Party with a spirit of cheerfulness and confidence in the victory of

* From: *Pravda,* March 2, 1930.

our cause. They bring forward additional millions of reserves for our Party.

Hence the Party's task is: to *consolidate* the successes achieved and to *utilize* them systematically for our further advancement.

But successes have their seamy side, especially when they are attained with comparative "ease"—"unexpectedly," so to speak. Such successes sometimes induce a spirit of vanity and conceit. "We can achieve anything!", "There's nothing we can't do!" People not infrequently become intoxicated by such successes; they become dizzy with success, lose all sense of proportion and the capacity to understand realities; they show a tendency to overrate their own strength and to underrate the strength of the enemy; adventurist attempts are made to solve all questions of socialist construction "in a trice." In such a case, there is no room for concern to *consolidate* the successes achieved and to *utilize* them systematically for further advancement. Why should we consolidate the successes achieved when, as it is, we can dash to the full victory of socialism "in a trice": "We can achieve anything!", "There's nothing we can't do!"

Hence the Party's task is: to wage a determined struggle against these sentiments, which are dangerous and harmful to our cause, and to drive them out of the Party.

It cannot be said that these dangerous and harmful sentiments are at all widespread in the ranks of our Party. But they do exist in our Party, and there are no grounds for asserting that they will not become stronger. And if they should be allowed free scope, then there can be no doubt that the collective-farm movement will be considerably weakened and the danger of its breaking down may become a reality.

— Reading No. 17 —

STALIN'S REPLY TO COLLECTIVE-FARM COMRADES*

First question: What is the *root* of the errors in the peasant question?

Reply: A wrong approach to the middle peasant. Resort to coercion in economic relations with the middle peasant. Forgetfulness of the fact that the economic bond with the masses of the middle peasants must be built not on the basis of coercive measures, but on the basis of agreement with the middle peasant, of alliance with him. Forgetfulness of the fact that the basis of the collective-farm movement at the present moment is an alliance of the working class and poor peasantry with the middle peasant against capitalism in general, against the kulaks in particular.

As long as the offensive against the kulak was waged in a united front with the middle peasant, all went well. But when some of our comrades became intoxicated with success and began imperceptibly to slip from the path of an offensive against the kulaks on to the path of a struggle against the middle peasant, when, in pursuit of high collectivization percentages, they began to apply coercion to the middle peasant, depriving him of the suffrage, "dekulakizing" and expropriating him, the offensive began to assume a distorted form and the united front with the middle peasant to be undermined, and, naturally, the kulak obtained an opportunity of trying to rise to his feet again.

* From: *Pravda,* April 3, 1930.

Second question: What are the chief errors in the collective-farm movement?

Reply: There are, at least, three such errors.

1) In building collective farms, Lenin's voluntary principle has been violated. The basic directives of the Party and the Model Rules of the Agricultural Artel about the voluntary character of collective-farm development have been violated. . . .

2) In building collective farms, Lenin's principle of taking into account the diversity of conditions in the various regions of the U.S.S.R. has been violated. It has been forgotten that in the U.S.S.R. there are the most diverse regions, with differing forms of economy and levels of culture. . . . It has been forgotten that rates of progress of the collective-farm movement and the methods of collective-farm development *cannot be uniform* in these far from uniform regions. . . .

3) In building collective farms, Lenin's principle that it is impermissible to skip over an uncompleted form of movement was violated. Also violated was Lenin's principle of not running ahead of the development of the masses, of not decreeing the movement of the masses, of not becoming divorced from the masses, but of moving together with the masses and impelling them forward, bringing them to our slogans and helping them to convince themselves of the correctness of our slogans through their own experience.

Third question. How could these errors have arisen, and how must the Party correct them?

Reply. They arose because of our rapid successes in the collective-farm movement. Success sometimes turns people's heads. It not infrequently gives rise to extreme vanity and conceit. That may very easily happen to representatives of a party which is in power, especially in the case of a party like ours, whose strength and prestige are almost immeasurable. Here, instances of communist vainglory, which Lenin combated so vehemently, are quite possible. Here, belief in the omnipotence of decrees, resolutions and orders is quite possible. Here, there is a real danger of the Party's revolutionary measures being converted into empty bureaucratic decreeing by individual representatives of the Party in one corner or another of our boundless country. I have in mind not only local officials, but also individual regional officials, and even individual members of the Central Committee.

Signed: J. STALIN

— Reading No. 18 —

FROM THE 1936 SOVIET CONSTITUTION*

Article 5.—Socialist property in the USSR exists either in the form of state property (belonging to the whole people) or in the form of co-operative and collective-farm property (property of collective farms, property of co-operative societies).

Article 6.—The land, its mineral wealth, waters, forests, mills, factories, mines, rail, water and air transport, banks, communications, large state-organized agricultural enterprises (state farms, machine and tractor stations and the like), as well as municipal enterprises and the bulk of the dwelling-houses in the cities and industrial localities, are state property, that is, belonging to the whole people.

Article 8.—The land occupied by collective farms is secured to them for their use free of charge and for an unlimited time, that is, in perpetuity.

Article 9.—Along side the socialist system of economy, which is the predominant form of economy in the USSR, the law permits the small private economy of individual peasants and handicraftsmen based on their own labor and precluding the exploitation of the labor of others.

* Official translation.

Article 10.—The personal property right of citizens in their incomes and savings from work, in their dwelling-houses and subsidiary husbandries, in articles of domestic economy and use and articles of personal use and convenience, as well as the right of citizens to inherit personal property, is protected by law.

Article 11.—The economic life of the USSR is determined and directed by the state of national-economic plan, with the aim of increasing the public wealth, of steadily raising the material and cultural standards of the working people, of consolidating the independence of the USSR and strengthening its defensive capacity.

Article 118.—Citizens of the USSR have the right to work, that is, the right to guaranteed employment and payment for their work in accordance with its quantity and quality.

The right to work is ensured by the socialist organization of the national economy, the steady growth of the productive forces of Soviet soicety, the elimination of the possibility of economic crises, and the abolition of unemployment.

— Reading No. 19 —

COLLECTIVE FARMS OF THE USSR, 1929-1940*

Year	No. of collective farms in 1000's	Sown area of collective farms mill. hectares	% of collective sown area serviced by MTS
1929	57.0	4.2	—
1930	85.9	38.1	27.4
1931	211.1	79.0	37.1
1932	211.1	91.5	49.3
1933	224.6	93.6	58.7
1934	233.3	98.6	63.9
1935	245.4	104.5	72.4
1936	242.2	110.5	82.8
1937	243.7	116.0	91.2
1938	242.4	117.2	93.3
1939	241.1	114.9	94.0
1940	236.3†	117.6	94.5

† The decrease in the numbers of collective farms from 1935 was due to the merging of small collective farms in a number of districts.

* From: A. Baykov. *The Development of the Soviet Economic System: An Essay on the Experience of Planning in the USSR.* The National Institute of Economic and Social Research and Cambridge University Press, 1946. Page 327.

— Reading No. 20 —

CATEGORIES OF STATE FARMS IN 1938 IN ACCORDANCE WITH THE NATURE OF THEIR FARMING*

	No.	% of total
State farms growing grain (including those growing seed)	471	11.7
State farms growing sugar beet	180	4.5
State farms growing special crops (tea, tobacco, rubber-bearing plants, etc.)	100	2.5
State farms growing potatoes, chicory and hops	77	1.9
State farms growing fibrous plants	63	1.6
State farms growing fruit and grapes	407	10.2
State farms breeding horses	119	3.0
State farms breeding cattle	755	18.9
State farms breeding pigs	650	16.3
State farms breeding sheep	200	5.0
State farms breeding reindeer and fur animals	39	1.0
State farms breeding poultry	95	2.4
Suburban and miscellaneous State farms	836	21.0
Total	3,992	100.0

* From: A. Baykov. *The Development of the Soviet Economic System: An Essay on the Experience of Planning in the USSR*. The National Institute of Economic and Social Research and Cambridge University Press, 1946. Page 334.

— Reading No. 21 —

COMPARATIVE OUTPUT AND TARGETS OF SOME LEADING PRODUCTS 1928-1942*

	1928	1938	1940	Target for 1942 Under 3rd Five Year Plan
Pig-iron, m. tons	3.3	14.6	15.0	22
Steel, m. tons	4.3	18	18.3	27.5
Rolled steel, m. tons	3.4	13.3	—	21
Coal, m. tons	35.5	133	166	243
Oil, m. tons	11.7	32	31	54
Electricity, md. kwt	5	39	48	75
Copper, 1000 tons	19.1	83.7	107†	—
Cement, m. tons	1.8	5.7	—	11
Railway locomotives	478	1626	—	2340
Tractors, 1000's	1.2	80**	—	—
Motor vehicles, 1000's	.7	211	—	400
Grain, m. tons	73	95	119	130
Sugar, 1000 tons	1283	2519	—	3500
Cotton cloth, m. metres	2742	3491	—	4900
Woolen cloth, m. metres	93	114	—	177
Leather footwear, m. pairs	29.6	213	—	258

† For 1939.
** For 1937.

* Cited by Maurice Dobb. *Soviet Economic Development Since 1917*. New York, International Publishers, 1948. Page 311.

— Reading No. 22 —

FROM THE REPORT OF THE CENTRAL COMMITTEE TO THE XX CONGRESS OF THE CPSU, DELIVERED BY N. S. KHRUSHCHEV, FIRST SECRETARY OF THE COMMUNIST PARTY, HELD ON FEBRUARY 14-25, 1946*

II. Our Domestic Position

INDUSTRY AND TRANSPORT

1. Despite the stride made towards communism in the 1951-5 plan, our basic economic aim—to overtake the leading capitalist countries in output per head of population—still requires much exertion. The party directs attention to technological innovation as the key to advance in the present phase, and to the comforts of routine as the chief obstacle.

2. Accelerated technical progress requires far more specialization of factories than hitherto and greater efforts in the machinery, power and metallurgical industries. But these and other capital industries are now sufficiently developed to permit a great extension in consumer goods, the annual output of which will by 1960 be nearly treble that of 1950.

3. The chief need of the railway is electrification, and the Central Committee has accepted a 15-year plan covering 25,000 miles of line. The chief immediate need in

* From: *Soviet Studies*, July 1956. Pages 85-87. Reprinted by permission of the publisher, Basil Blackwell, Oxford.

road transport is to pool the use of lorries and official cars.

4. A new scale of development in the coal and power, metallurgy and engineering of our Asiatic territories, Siberia especially, is now possible and necessary.

5. As ever, productivity in industry is the chief economic and political criterion of our progress. The amount of construction is now so great that productivity in building is assuming a new importance.

AGRICULTURE

The large investments made in 1954-5 and the higher prices, new cadres and decentralized planning for the collective farms are already showing some good results.

1. More fodder grain is the first necessity for more protein foods. Large areas good for fodder maize will be freed of wheat by the pioneering of the virgin and abandoned lands. The youth movement did this pioneering very much more quickly and cheaply than would be possible by the normal method of family migration, and we shall, during the present five-year plan, be making more such appeals to the youth for *industrial* pioneering of remote areas.

2. The new livestock incentives are showing good results (too good, in the cases where human food is being bought in the shops by farms as feed!), but this improvement is only a beginning in a most difficult and urgent undertaking.

3. The Machine Tractor Stations, hitherto financed by the state independently of their efficiency, must each be put on a profit-and-loss basis. The farms need lighter tractors properly adapted to local conditions in many areas; tractor-mounted instead of trailer implements; and an effective national policy of rural electrification.

4. State farms (which are of course the most socialist type of agricultural organization) have increased in number by the virgin lands' development.

5. Our seed supply is badly organized. We are having to buy hybrid maize seed from American firms, and should emulate their excellent organization of its production.

6. The cash incomes of many farms and farmers are

now rising beyond the age-old poverty level of their housing and amenities. The state should facilitate but not pay for rehousing. Collective farms should be allowed to join together to finance and control district brick-works and building firms. Agricultural efficiency requires decent housing, amenities and roads.

7. Most of the central and local staff of the three agricultural ministries, watching over and in the collective farms, are unnecessary. Collective farm efficiency, which varies very widely, depends on the competence of the farms' own managers and technicians.

American farms, so much more efficient than ours, are ruthlessly capitalist. Our output per farm worker will in due course exceed theirs but even then our agricultural population may well be larger, because our farms, being collectives, support their own sick and aged members. Meanwhile, we must study and emulate foreign agricultural efficiency.

CONSUMPTION AND CULTURE

1. Order is being established in the wages system, on our traditional and justifiable principle of wide differentials, but the lowest earnings (and pensions) are being raised and the highest reduced. We propose to replace the present working week of six-hour days by a working week of five 7-hour days and one 6-hour day or five 8-hour days with two days off.

Our urban housing effort, now large, is nullified in the great towns by the immigrant flood, which should be replaced by increased productivity. Satellite towns should be built around the great towns, and individual house-building should be encouraged more. The following need special expansion and improvement: public catering, which should be made cheaper than home-cooking; the supply of domestic electrical appliances; school meals, which are to be free for low incomes; rural health services. But there is no aspect of the standard of living that is not in urgent need of very great efforts.

DJILAS ON PLANNED ECONOMY*

A severe critic of Communism, Milovan Djilas, is much less enthusiastic about "planned economy" and has this to say on the subject:

↗   ↗   ↗

Soviet, or Communist, planning is of a special kind. It has not evolved as the result of the technological development of production nor as the result of the "socialist" consciousness of its initiators. Instead it has evolved as the result of a special type of government and ownership. Today, technical and other factors are also in operation, but the factors mentioned above have not ceased to operate. It is very important to note this, for it is the key to understanding the character of this type of planning, and of the capabilities of a Communist economy.

The results achieved by such an economy and by such planning are varied. The concentration of all means to achieve a specific purpose make it possible for the power-wielders to progress with extraordinary speed in certain branches of the economy. The progress that the U.S.S.R. has achieved in some branches has heretofore never been achieved anywhere in the world. However, when one considers the backward conditions existing in other branches the progress achieved is not justified from the over-all economic point of view.

Of course, once-backward Russia has attained second place in world production as far as its most important branches of the economy are concerned. It has become

* From: Milovan Djilas. *The New Class. An Analysis of the Communist System.* New York: Frederick A. Praeger, 1957. Pages 117-122.

the mightiest continental power in the world. A strong working class, a wide stratum of technical intelligentsia, and the materials for consumer goods production have been created. The dictatorship has not been essentially weakened because of this, nor are there any reasons to believe that the standard of living cannot be improved in proportion to the country's economic capabilities.

Ownership and political considerations for which the plan is only an implement have made it impossible to weaken the dictatorship to any extent or to raise the standard of living. The exclusive monopoly of a single group, in the economy as well as in politics, planning that is directed toward increasing its power and its interests in the country and throughout the world, continuously postpones the improvement of the standard of living and harmonious development of the economy. The absence of freedom is undoubtedly the final and most important reasons for the postponement. In Communist systems freedom has become the main economic and general problem.

The Communist planned economy conceals within itself an anarchy of a special kind. In spite of the fact that it is planned, the Communist economy is perhaps the most wasteful economy in the history of human society. Such claims may seem strange, especially if one has in mind the relatively rapid development of individual branches of the economy, and of the economy as a whole. However, they have a solid basis.

Wastefulness of fantastic proportions was unavoidable even if this had not been a group which considered everything, including the economy, from its own narrow, ownership and ideological point of view. How could a single group of this kind administer a complex modern economy effectively and thriftily—an economy which, in spite of the most complete planning, showed varied and often contradictory internal and external tendencies from day to day? The absence of any type of criticism, even of any type of important suggestion, inevitably leads to waste and stagnation.

Because of this political and economic omnipotence, wasteful undertakings cannot be avoided even with the best of intentions. Very little attention is paid to what the cost of these undertakings is to the economy as a whole. How great are the costs to a nation of an agriculture which is stagnant because of the superstitious Communist fear of the peasant and unreasonable investments in heavy industry? What is the cost of capital invested in inefficient industries? What is the cost of a stagnant transportation system? What is the cost of poorly paid workers, who consequently "goldbrick" and work slowly? What is the cost of poor-quality production? There is no counting these costs, nor can they be calculated.

Just as they administer the economy, the Communist leaders handle everything in a way contrary to their own teaching: that is, from their personal viewpoint. The economy is just an area which least tolerates arbitrariness. Even if they wished to do so, the leaders could not fake into consideration the interests of the economy as a whole. For political reasons the ruling group determines what is 'vitally necessary', of "key importance," or "decisive" in a movement. Nothing stands in the way of its carrying out the matter in question, for the group is not afraid of losing its power or property.

Periodically the leaders indulge in criticism or self-criticism and cite experience when there is evidence that something is not progressing or when tremendous waste has become apparent. Khrushchev criticized Stalin for his agricultural policy. Tito criticized his own regime for excessive capital investments and the waste of billions. Ochab criticized himself for this "conditional" neglect of the standard of living. But the essence remains the same. The same men prolong the same system by about the same method, until breaches and 'irregularities' become apparent. Losses incurred can no longer be restored, so the regime and the party do not take the responsibility for the losses. They have "noted" the errors and these errors will be "corrected." So let's begin all over again!

There is no evidence that a single Communist leader has suffered because of unproductively expended or fantastically wasted means. But many have been deposed because of "ideological deviations."

In Communist systems, thefts and misappropriations are inevitable. It is not just poverty that motivates people to steal the "national property"; but the fact that the property does not seem to belong to anyone. All valuables are somehow rendered valueless, thus creating a favorable atmosphere for theft and waste. In 1954, in Yugoslavia alone, over 20,000 cases of theft of "socialist property" were discovered. The Communist leaders handle national property as their own, but at the same time they waste it as if it were somebody else's. Such is the nature of ownership and government of the system.

The greatest waste is not even visible. This is the waste of manpower. The slow, unproductive work of disinterested millions, together with the prevention of all work not considered "socialist," is the calculable, invisible, and gigantic waste which no Communist regime has been able to avoid. Even though they are adherents of Smith's theory that labor creates value, a theory which Marx adopted, these power-wielders pay the least attention to labor and manpower, regarding them as something of very little value which can be readily replaced.

The fear which Communists have of "the renewal of capitalism," or of economic consequences that would arise from narrow class "ideological" motives, has cost the nation tremendous wealth and put a brake on its development. Entire industries are destroyed because the state is not in a position to maintain or develop them; only that which is the state's is considered "socialist." . . .

The waste is tremendous because of the isolation of Communist economies. Every Communist economy is essentially autarchic. The reasons for this autarchy lie in the character of its government and ownership. . . .

Communist planning, among other things, takes very little account of the needs of world markets or of the production in other countries. Partly as a result of this, and partly as a result of ideological and other motives, Communist governments take too little account of national conditions affecting production. They often construct industrial plants without having sufficient raw materials available for them, and almost never pay attention to the world level of price and production. They produce some products at several times the production cost in other countries. Simultaneously, other branches of industry which could surpass the world average in productivity, or which could produce at lower prices than the world average, are neglected. Entire new industries are being developed, even though world markets are surfeited with the items they will produce. The working people have to pay for all this in order to make the oligarchs 'independent'.

This is one aspect of the problem common to Communist regimes. Another is the senseless race of the "leading Socialist country"—the U.S.S.R.—to overtake and pass the most highly developed countries. What does this cost? And where does it lead?

Perhaps the U.S.S.R. can overtake some branches of the economy of the most highly developed countries. By infinite waste of manpower, by low wages, and by neglect of the other branches of industry, this may be possible. It is quite another question whether this is economically justifiable.

— Reading No. 24 —

BASIC TASKS IN THE DEVELOPMENT OF THE NATIONAL ECONOMY OF THE USSR FROM 1959 TO 1965 *

1. The main task of the Seven Year Plan for the development of the national economy of the USSR in the period from 1959 to 1965 is a further mighty upsurge of all branches of the economy on the basis of priority for the expansion of heavy industry, and a substantial rise

* From: N. S. Khrushchev's Report to the Twenty-First Congress of the Communist Party of the Soviet Union. Pages 136-139.

in the country's economic potential so as to ensure a continuous improvement in the living standards of the people.

As a result of the fulfilment of this plan, a decisive step will be taken towards the creating the material and technical basis for communism and accomplishing the main economic task of the USSR: to overtake and surpass the most highly developed capitalist countries in output per head of the population within the shortest possible period of history.

The Communist Party considers it an all-important task to ensure, within this seven-year period, a further substantial growth of the real incomes of the population in town and countryside and a considerable rise in the wages for the lower and medium paid jobs of factory and office workers. The target figures for 1959-65 envisage a big expansion in the production and consumption of foodstuffs and manufactured goods. Housing construction will be developed on a big scale. . . .

2. For the sake of the greatest possible acceleration of the economic development of the USSR, the target figures provide for the priority growth of those branches of heavy industry which promote the further advance of the entire national economy. . . .

3. An important task of the forthcoming seven-year period is that of intensively exploiting the rich natural resources of our country, improving the distribution of the productive forces on its territory, and bringing industry still closer to the sources of raw materials and fuel and to the consumer areas.

Special attention is devoted to the further development of the natural resources of the eastern parts of the USSR. With this end in view, provision is made for:

Building a powerful metallurgical center—the third—on the basis of the new iron ore deposits discovered in recent years in Siberia and Kazakhstan. . . .

Extensively developing the power industry in Siberia on the basis of cheap coal from the new fields; . . .

Higher yields of agricultural crops and higher productivity of animal husbandry.

TARGET FIGURES FOR THE USSR'S ECONOMIC DEVELOPMENT FROM 1958 TO 1965*

	1958 expected fulfillment	1965	1965 percentage of 1958
Cotton fabrics (mill. metres†)	5,800	7,700-8,000	133-138
Woolen fabrics (mill. metres)	300	500	167
Linen fabrics (mill. metres)	480	635	132
Silk fabrics (mill. metres)	814	1,485	182
Hosiery (mill. pairs)	882	1,250	142
Knitted underwear (mill. items)	392	780	199
Knitted garments (mill. items)	95	160	168
Leather footwear (mill. pairs)	355	515	145
Meat, including first-category subsidiary products, from state raw material resources (thousand tons)	2,830	6,130	217
Butter from state raw material resources (thousand tons)	627	1,006	160
Dairy products, in terms of milk (thousand tons)	6,017	13,546	225

* From: *Soviet Seven Year Plan,* with Foreword by A. W. Haslett. London, Todd Reference Books, 1959.

152

	1958 expected fulfillment	1965	1965 percentage of 1958
Granulated sugar, from sugar beet (thousand tons)	5,150	9,250-10,000	180-194
Vegetable oil, from state raw material resources (thousand tons)	1,221	1,975	162
Fish catch (thousand tons)	2,850	4,626	162
Ethyl alcohol (million decalitres**) including alcohol made from edible raw material (million decalitres)	111.7	100	90

† One metre = 1.09 yard
** One decalitre = 2.2 gallons

— Reading No. 26 —

TARGET FIGURES OF BASIC AGRICULTURAL PRODUCTS TO BE INCREASED BY 1965 *

	1965 (thousand tons)	1965 in percentage of 1957
Raw cotton	5,700 = 6,100	135-145
Sugar beet	70,000-78,000	180-200
Oil-bearing seeds	3,560	180
Potatoes	11,720	148
Flax fibre	530	137
Meat	11,050	120
Milk	40,610	100
Wool	540	90
Eggs (in mill.)	10,000	130

* From: *Soviet Seven Year Plan,* with Foreword by A. W. Haslett. London, Todd Reference Books, 1959.

— Reading No. 27 —

TARGET FIGURES FOR THE USSR'S ECONOMIC DEVELOPMENT FROM 1959 TO 1965 *

	1965	Increases in percentages of 1958
Metal-cutting machine tools (thousands)	190-200	40-50
Including special, specialized and aggregate machine tools (thousands)	38	100
Forge and pressing machines (thousands)	36.2	50
Automatic and semi-automatic machine lines (complete sets)	250-271	90-110
Precision instruments (million rubles	18,500-19,200	150-160
Including computers and mathematical machines (million rubles)	2,000	350-370
Turbines (million kW)	18.7-20.4	180-200
Generators for turbines (million kW)	17.5-18.4	230-200
Electric motors—alternating current (million kW)	32-34	120-140
Rolling mill equipment (thousand tons)	200-220	100-120
Chemical equipment (million rubles)	3,500-3,700	230-250

* From: *Soviet Seven Year Plan*, with Foreword by A. W. Haslett. London, Todd Reference Books, 1959.

	1965	Increases in percentages of 1958
Technological equipment for the textile industry (mill. rubles)	2,500	120
Technological equipment for the food and flour industries (million rubles)	3,800-4,100	110-130
Motor vehicles (thousands)	730-856	50-70
Trunk-line, electric and diesel locomotive (units) (million h.p.)	2,550-2,700 8.4-9.0	130-150 180-200
Technological equipment for the cement industry (thousand tons)	180-220	110-160
Technological equipment for foundry production (mill. rubles)	360-510	100-130

— Reading No. 28 —

REVISED TARGETS FOR BASIC PRODUCTION, 1964-1965 †

	1958	1962	1965 Old Plan	New Plan
Coal, mill. tons	496	517	600-612	553
Crude oil, mill. tons	113	186	230-240	240
Natural gas, bill. cub. metres	30	75	150	128
Electric power	235	369	500-520	508
Pig iron, mill. tons	39.6	55.3	65-70*	65.7
Crude steel, mill. tons	54.9	76.3	86-81**	89.3

* Revised in 1961 to 72-73 mill. tons.
** Revised in 1961 to 95-97 mill. tons.

† From: *The Economist,* January 18, 1964. Page 190.

— Reading No. 29 —

ON THE DEVELOPMENT OF
THE VIRGIN LANDS*

The development of virgin and disused lands is prominent among the measures implemented by the Party. The Central Committee is happy to report to the Congress that this task has been successfully accomplished. In the boundless steppes of Kazakhstan, Siberia, the Volga region, the Urals and other eastern areas, 41,800,000 hectares of land have been cultivated and put at the service of the people. The new lands now account for over 40 percent of the grain purchased by the state. *Their development is a great feat which our heroic people have performed in building communism. It is an achievement that will live through the ages.*

The newly-developed lands have radically changed the grain balance of many areas of our country. It is with pride and elation that we speak of this historic fact—the increase in the country's grain output achieved through the development of new lands. Before the new lands were developed, the regions concerned produced an annual average of 1,386 million poods† of grain; between 1956 and 1960, their output averaged 3,363 million poods a year.

* From *The Road to Communism. Documents of the 22nd Congress of the Communist Party of the Soviet Union, October 17-31, 1961.* Moscow, Foreign Languages Publishing House.

† One pood = 36 lbs.

— Reading No. 30 —

CONFUSION DUE TO CENTRALIZATION*

The Oktyabrski state farm of Pavlodar Oblast needs a flax thresher about as much as a fish needs an umbrella. Flax has never been sown in these regions and is not now sown there. Or why does the "Chekhov" grain state farm receive all at once 136 tractor-operated reapers? Yet the state farm was compelled not only to accept the reapers but also to pay 644,000 rubles for them. In vain it begged: "Take away these reapers, pass them on to someone who needs them."

— Reading No. 31 —

OBJECTIONS TO REORGANIZATION†

. . . The idea still exists among us that it is possible to solve intricate economic problems through administrative measures; all one has to do is to reorganize the apparatus, merge two administrations into one or, conversely, divide one trust into two, and everything will be fine. This is a most fallacious approach.

* From: *Krokodil,* June 10, 1950.
† From: *Pravda,* November 1, 1964.

— Reading No. 32 —

PRODUCTION PROBLEMS*

Major problems of social production remain unsolved in the maze of innumerable specific problems. For example, many measures envisaged by the plans are not corroborated by economic efficiency calculations. Frequently it turns out that material and technical supplies and particularly financial tasks are not coordinated with production programs. Quite frequently the plans are disseminated down to the plants only in February or March of the planned year, but nevertheless they must be constantly corrected. Thus, if all the changes which were effected in the plans of the Moscow City Sovnarkhoz in the past few years were summed up, it turns out that one task or another, on the average, changed almost daily. Because of its unwieldiness the plan to a considerable extent loses its guiding role.

* From: *Special Information Note*, No. 69, January 18, 1965.

LIBERMAN ON PROFIT UNDER COMMUNISM *

LENIN'S IDEA OF COST ACCOUNTING

In the western press there were no few conjectures that the use of the criteria of profit and profitability in the USSR amounts almost to a repudiation of building communist society and a return to capitalism. But in making their conjectures they fail to explain that it is not simply today that Soviet economists have invented or recommended profit. It was none other than Lenin, the founder of the Soviet state, who insisted that socialist enterprises should cover their outlays from their profit and leave a profit for society. And it was he who maintained that communism could not be built on enthusiasm alone, but on enthusiasm coupled with personal material interest—an operation on a paying basis. The use of the criteria of profit and profitability is therefore the consistent introduction of Lenin's principles of cost accounting of socialist enterprises in the system of economic management of production.

In the Soviet Union profit is not invented at will by any individuals or groups of individuals for the purpose of deriving private income. It belongs to those who own the means of production, to society as a whole. All profit goes for planned expansion and improvement of production, for free social services to the population. A certain portion is spent to maintain the government apparatus, and, unfortunately, for the time being no small portion to meet the needs of the country's defense. We would

* From: "Profit as the Servant of Communism." By Evsei Liberman. *The Economist,* February 26, 1966. Page 786.

gladly give up defence spending if a general disarmament programme was adopted.

For a long time the USSR stood alone and our people had to develop industry and provide for their defense in the shortest possible time at any price. At that time we often had to forget quality or the appearance of articles or even the cost price. But, as Lenin said more than once, if virtues are exaggerated they may turn into vices. Something of this nature occurred when the methods of running the economy I have described were continued in many sectors even when the USSR had entered the period of the comprehensive building of communist society.

The question raised is not to slacken planning but to improve it in every way. Direct contractual relations with consumers or customers do not at all mean a transition to market regulation. In the capitalist world too they try to foresee consumer demand. But in our country we can probably do it better, as the wage fund of the urban population and the income of collective farmers are known, and we therefore can make up well-founded balance sheets of the population's income and expenditures. The total volume of consumer demand is a fully plannable figure, but concretely how the volume is to be made up, what color a blouse should come in, or what style suits should be made, should not be decided by means of central planning, but should be agreed upon between stores and factories. Thus, calculating the population's demand and planning production are not only compatible but should substantiate and supplement each other.

— Reading No. 34 —

REPORT OF THE CENTRAL STATISTICAL BOARD OF THE USSR ON THE RESULTS OF THE FULFILMENT OF THE STATE NATIONAL ECONOMIC DEVELOPMENT PLAN IN 1965 *

The development of the economy and the improvement in the living standards of the Soviet people over the past year, the concluding year of the seven-year-plan period, are characterized by the following data:

	1965 as percentage of 1964
Social product (output of all the branches of material production)	c. 107
National income	106
Fixed production assets in the national economy at the end of the year	110
Total industrial output, including	
Department 1	108.7
Department 2	108.5
Agricultural output	101
Freight output (all means of transportation)	110
Retail goods turnover	110
Labor productivity:	

* From: *Pravda,* February 3, 1966, and *Moscow News,* February 12, 1966.

Data on plan fulfilment by individual branches of the national economy follow below.

I. Industry

The year's plan for the general volume of production and for the output of key items has been overfulfilled in all the Union Republics and in the USSR as a whole.

In the past seven years industrial output grew 84 per cent as against 80 per cent provided for by the Seven Year Plan. Altogether, 46 thousand million roubles' worth of above-plan output was produced in seven years.

The output of individual industries increased as follows in comparison with the previous year.

Electric and thermal power   111
Fuel industry   107
Ferrous & non-ferrous metallurgy   109

Chemical industry 114
Machine-building & metal-working 109
Timber, woodworking, pulp & paper industries 104
Building material industry 109
Light and food industry 108
Cultural goods & household appliances 110

The industrial output of enterprises coming under some
of the Ministries increased as follows:

USSR Ministry of Power & Electrification ... 112
USSR Oil-Extracting Industry 109
USSR Oil Refining & Petro-Chemical Industry 111
Ministry of the Gas Industry 116
USSR Ministry of the Coal Industry 105
USSR Ministry of the Ferrous Metallurgy .. 107
USSR Ministry of the Non-Ferrous Metallurgy 111
USSR Ministry of the Chemical Industry 116
Ministry of Heavy, Power & Transport
   Engineering 107
Ministry of the Electrical Engineering Industry 111
Ministry of the Apparatus, Automation &
   Control-System Manufacturing Industry ... 112
Ministry of the Machine-Tool & Instrument-
   Making Industry 109
Ministry of Chemical & Oil Engineering 110
Ministry of the Construction, Road Building
   & Municipal Machine-Building Industry ... 111
Ministry of the Automobile Industry 110
Ministry of the Tractor & Agricultural
   Machinery Industry 108
Ministry of Machine-Building for the Light &
   Food Industry & Household Appliances ... 112
USSR Ministry of the Timber, Pulp & Paper,
   & Woodworking Industry 105
USSR Ministry of the Building Materials
   Industry 109
USSR Ministry of the Light Industry 100.5
USSR Ministry of the Food Industry 111
USSR Ministry of the Meat & Dairy Industry . 123
USSR Ministry of Fisheries 103
USSR Ministry of Health 111

The output of the individual types of industrial goods came to:

	Produced in 1965	1965 as percentage of 1964
Electric power (1000 millions of kw. hours)	507	110
Oil (million tons)	243	109
Gas (1000 million cubic metres) ..	129	117
Coal (million tons)	578	104
Including coal for coking	139	104
Pig iron (million tons)	66.2	106
Steel (million tons)	91	107
Rolled metal, total (mill. tons) ..	70.9	106
Including finished rolled goods (pipe & forgings of ingots and billets to be re-rolled at other plants)	61.6	107
Steel piping		
million meters	1,382	108
thousand tons	9,013	111
Iron ore (mill. tons)	153	105
Mineral fertilizers (mill. tons) in terms of 100% content of nutritious substances	7.4	123
In conventional units	31.3	122
Chemical means of plant protection in terms of agent content (1000 tons)	103	121
Sulphuric acid (1000 tons)	8,518	111
Synthetic resins & plastics (1000 tons)	821	114
Chemical fibres (1000 tons)	407	113
Caustic soda (1000 tons)	1,303	113
Soda ash (million tons)	2.9	105
Motor tires	26.4	109
Turbines (mill. kw.)	14.6	110
Generators for turbines (mill. kw.)	14.4	112
A.C. electric motors (mill. kw.) ..	29.6	103
Metal-cutting machine tools (1000's)	185	100.4

Automatic & semi-automatic production lines for machine building & metal-processing (sets) ..	218	95
Instruments (1000 mill. roubles)..	2.1	111
Metallurgical equipment (1000 tons)	243	100.8
Oil industry equipment (1000 tons)	140	100
Chemical industry equipment (million roubles)	384	112
Looms (thousands)	24.3	98
Trunk-line Diesel engine locomotives (sections)	1,485	100.1
Trunk-line electric locomotives ...	641	100.5
Automobiles (1000's)	616	102
Including: trucks & buses	415	99.3
Cars	201	109
Tractors (1000's)	355	108
Agricultural machines total (mill. roubles)	1,431	103
Tractor-drawn ploughs (1000's) ..	166	93
Tractor-drawn sowing machines (1000's)	262	111
Tractor-drawn cultivators (1000's) .	206	107
Tractor-drawn mowers (1000's) ..	122	113
Combines (1000's):		
grain combines	85.8	103
beet-picking combines	17.5	96
Cotton pickers (1000's)	7.7	111
Windrowers (1000's)	97.8	117
Grain cleaners (1000's)	24.1	99.6
Excavators (1000's)	21.6	107
Commercial timber, excluding timber cut by collective farms (mill. cubic meters)	258	99
Paper (million tons)	3.4	112
Cement (million tons)	72.4	111
Pre-cast reinforced concrete (million cubic meters)	56	112
Building bricks, excluding collective farm production (1000 mill.)	34	101
State farm production (1000 mill conventional units)	4.2	104

Soft roofing (mill. sq. meters)	1,080	109
Window glass (mill. sq. meters) ...	190	102
Fabrics (mill. sq. meters):		
cotton	5,504	102
woolen	466	99
linen	547	100.7
silk	796	96
Garments (1000 mill. roubles) ...	9.3	99.9
Knitted underwear (millions)	719	112
Knitted outer garments (millions)	188	123
Leather footwear (mill. pairs)	486	102
Meat, total (mill. tons)	9.6	116
Including industrial production	5.2	125
Sausage (million tons)	1.6	107
Fish & sea food (mill. tons)	5.7	112
Butter, total (1000 tons)	1,184	124
Excluding collective farms and individual household productions	1,070	127
Wholemilk produce in terms of milk (milk, curds, kefir, sour milk, cream, sour cream, cream cheese, etc.), excluding collective farm and individual household production (million tons)	11.7	112
Cheese, excluding collective farms & individual household production (1000 tons)	288	113
Granulated sugar, total (mill. tons)	11.0	134
Including sugar made of sugar beet	8.9	127
Confectionery (mill. tons)	2.3	100.6
Vegetable oil, excluding collective farm & individual household production (mill. tons)	2.7	124
Tinned goods (1000 mill. cans) ..	7.0	94
Soap & detergents (mill. tons)	1.9	103
Clocks & watches (millions)	30.6	107
Radios & phonographs (millions)..	5.2	108
Television sets (millions)	3.7	125
Refrigerators (thousands)	1,675	148
Washing machines (millions)	3.4	120

Motorcycles & motor scooters (thousands)	721	105
Bicycles & motorbikes (mill.)	3.9	107
Furniture (1000 mill. roubles)	1.8	108

There has also been an increase in the output of non-ferrous metals, synthetic rubber and ammonia, products of oil processing and petro-chemistry and many other types of produce.

The country's research, planning and designing organizations and industrial enterprises continued their work on bringing new machinery and advanced technology into production. About 3,000 new models of machines, mechanisms, apparatuses and other equipment and more than 1,100 various new types of instruments for the control and automation of production were designed and manufactured in the course of the year. The country's industrial enterprises have mastered the production of about 900 new items, including powerful units and sets of machines for the power industry and coal mines, highly efficient machine tools and automatic lines, agricultural machines, powerful trucks, new types of synthetic rubber, chemical fibre, fertilizers as well as new types of consumer goods and cultural utility goods. At the same time the production of some 400 obsolete types of machines, equipment and instruments has been discontinued.

In the past year about 2,800,000 inventions and rationalization proposals for the technical improvement and modernization of production were introduced into the national economy.

The annual plan for raising labor productivity and reducing the cost price of industrial produce has been fulfilled; profits have grown. The above-plan saving due to the reduction of the production costs was about 250 million roubles.

Besides the achievements, there were also some shortcomings in the work of industry. Many enterprises failed to achieve their targets for output growth of labor productivity, reduction of costs and for accumulations. Though there was a general growth of production, the plan for the output of chemical means of plant-protection, sulphuric acid, chemical fibre, caustic soda, turbines, metal-cutting machines, chemical equipment, paper, bricks, soft roofing, window glass, radio sets and radiograms, TV sets, refrigerators, bicycles and motorbikes has been somewhat underfulfilled. The output of produce per rouble of the fixed production in considerable measure with the slow progress in the slow mastering of the production capacities commissioned, particularly in the iron and steel industry, in the coal, chemical and pulp and paper industries and in the building-materials industry. The required improvement was not achieved in the utilization of equipment at some of the machine-building enterprises. The plan for research work and the introduction of the achievements of science and technology in the national economy has been underfulfilled.

II. Agriculture

On the basis of the decisions of the March 1965 CPSU Central Committee Plenary Meeting important measures were taken to develop agriculture and further strengthen the economy of the collective and state farms.

According to preliminary data, the volume of agricultural production in 1965 was somewhat greater than the highest level of agricultural production reached in the preceding year. There was a substantial increase in the output of livestock produce, while the output of crops was lower than in 1964.

Last year the prices for some of the agricultural products purchased by the state in the collective farms and for the products coming from the state farms were increased. As compared to the preceding year, the gross income of collective farms increased by 16 per cent. There was a corresponding increase in the amount of money paid to the collective farmers for their work. The issue of grain as payment in kind for the work done increased by 7 per cent.

There was a growth in the number of state farms which showed a profit at the end of the year. However, not all farms have reached an adequate level of profitability.

In crop-farming the drought in the country's eastern areas result in a reduction in the gross grain harvest, which amounted to 120.5 million tons in 1965. The volume of grain purchases was less than envisaged by the plan. As a result of the measures taken, the country's requirements in grain products are fully ensured.

Grain purchases were conducted with the procedure established by the March Plenary Meeting of the CPSU Central Committee. The collective and state farms set aside approximately the same amount of grain as in 1964 for their own needs.

There was an increase in the production of cereals. Rice production increased by 21 per cent as compared with the preceding year and buckwheat by 32 per cent. There was a considerable increase in state purchases of these products.

Great successes have been attained in cotton growing. The country received 5.7 million tons of raw cotton, i.e., more than ever before.

A good crop of sugar-beet, sunflower seed, flax, potatoes and other vegetables was harvested.

At the same time a number of collective and state farms are slow in tackling problems concerning a rise in agricultural efficiency, as a result of which agricultural crop yields remain low.

Preparations are under way on collective and state farms for the spring sowing campaign. The plan for autumn ploughing for the 1966 harvest has been fulfilled. More tractors and other machines have been repaired than envisaged by the plan for the fourth quarter of 1965.

There has been an improvement in animal husbandry. The increase of young stock on the collective and state farms over the 1964 figure (per 100 of mature female stock) was: calves—by 14 per cent, piglets—by 20 per cent, lambs and young goats—also 20 per cent. There has been an increase in livestock productivity. The average milk yield increased by 18 per cent. The average weight of livestock sold to the state increased as follows: cattle—by 11 per cent, pigs—by 14 per cent.

The productive livestock population in the country is as follows:

The plan for purchasing livestock produce was fulfilled ahead of schedule.

Along with definite successes achieved in developing animal husbandry, there are as yet considerable shortcomings. On a number of farms work is being inadequately conducted in setting up a reliable fodder base, there is a considerable dearth of cows, a loss in young stock and low productivity of livestock.

The strengthening of the material and technical basis of agricultural production continued. During the past year a large program of capital construction was carried out in agriculture; capital investments made by the state and by collective farms amounted to more than 11,000 million roubles. During the year agriculture obtained 240,000 tractors in physical units or 483,000 in terms of 15 horse-power units, more than 77,000 trucks, 77,000 grain harvesting combines, 22,000 silo harvestors, 17,000 beet pullers, 6,000 potato harvesters, 95,000 windrowers and 8,000 cotton pickers. A large number of tractor-mounted or trailer machines was also delivered, including 157,000 ploughs, 253,000 seeders, 205,000 cultivators, 43,000 stubble breakers, 118,000 mowers, 35,000 mineral fertilizer distributors, 21,000 herbicide-ammonia distributors, 68,000 multi-purpose loaders and a large number of other farming machines and equipment. The supply of mineral fertilizers increased by 23 per cent.

III. Transport

Transport in the USSR has been further developed, ensuring the needs of the national economy in carrying freight.

The following figures show the fulfillment of plan by the various branches of transport:

	Number of livestock at the end of the year (million head)		1965 as percentage of 1964
	1964	1965	
All categories of farms			
Cattle	87.2	93.4	107
Of which cows	38.8	40.1	103.5
Pigs	52.8	59.5	113
Sheep & goats	130.7	135.3	103.5

	Number of livestock at the end of the year (million head)		1965 as percentage of 1964
	1964	1965	
Collective farms, state farms & other state enterprises			
Cattle	62.1	65.5	106
Of which cows	22.6	23.5	104
Pigs	38.3	41.3	108
Sheep & goats	100.2	103.1	103

On the basis of the increase in productivity and the growth in the livestock population, there has been a rise in the output of animal products:

	Output of animal products in all categories of farms		1965 as percentage of 1964
	1964	1965	
Meat, in slaughter weight (million tons)	8.3	9.6	116
Milk (million tons)	63.3	72.4	114
Eggs (1000 millions) . .	26.7	29.0	109
Wool (thousand tons) . .	341	356	104

Increase in State Purchases of Livestock Produce

	Purchase of livestock produce in all categories of farms		1965 as percentage of 1964
	1964	1965	
Cattle and poultry (million tons):			
Live weight	8.3	9.3	112
In terms of slaughter weight	5.0	5.7	116
Milk (mill. tons)	31.4	38.7	123
Eggs (1,000 millions) . .	8.3	10.5	126

Freight turnover (in 1,000 million ton-kilometers)

	Fulfilment in 1965	Percentage fulfilment of 1965 plan	1965 as percentage of 1964
Railways	1,948	103	105
Public river transport ..	134	103	108
Public motor transport .	42	104	109
Oil pipelines	147	99	131
Freight traffic (in million tons)			
Railways	2,401	102	106
Public rivers transport ..	269	106	107
Public motor transport .	2,353	102	106
Oil pipelines	226	103	106

Marine transport has overfulfilled the annual plan for shipping in respect to both coastal and deep sea operations. Marine cargo turnover as a whole increased 30 per cent and freight shipping 9 per cent. The assignment on raising labor productivity and lowering transportation costs has been fulfilled.

Air transport has overfulfilled its plan. As compared with the previous year the air-passenger turnover increased 23 per cent and freight turnover 19 per cent; passenger air traffic increased 14 per cent and freight carriage 12 per cent.

During last year freight turnover on all types of transport went up 10 per cent, and in the course of the seven-year plan period 72 per cent as compared to 56-59 per cent provided for by the plan.

Profit derived by all types of transport increased 10 per cent.

In the course of the year the length of railway lines converted to electric and diesel traction increased by 8,000 kilometers and is now nearly 80,000 kilometers in all.

Electric and diesel traction accounted for 85 per cent of the overall railway freight turnover, i.e., it achieved the level provided for in the Seven-Year Plan.

Targets were reached in respect to cutting down turnover time, cutting down rolling stock idle time, increasing section (commercial) speed of freight trains, the average daily run of locomotives, average weight of trains, raising labor productivity and lower transportation costs. However, some railways fell short of targets in respect to certain indices pertaining to the utilization of rolling stock.

Idle time and idle runs in marine, river and motor transport have been reduced insufficiently and are still high.

IV. Capital Construction

In the past year new production capacities were put into operation in all branches of the national economy. Some 500 major industrial enterprises as well as a large number of new shops and production lines at enterprises undergoing reconstruction and expansion were commissioned.

The following data characterize the commissioning of production capacities.

	Capacities commissioned in 1965
Power stations (million kw.)	over 11
Coal (million tons)	11.4
Steel (million tons)	1.8
Rolled stock (million tons)	1.4
Iron ore (million tons)	28
Mineral fertilizers (million tons) ...	7.1
Synthetic resins & plastics (1000 tons)	120
Chemical fibres (millions)	66
Automobile tires (millions)	3.3
Chemical equipment (million roubles)	52
Cement (million tons)	4.9
Paper (thousand tons)	510
Looms (thousands)	12
Leather footwear (million pairs) ...	12.5
Granulated sugar (1000 centners of sugar-beet processed daily)	278
Refrigeration capacities (1000 tons)	270

Trunk-line pipeline (1000 kilometers)	5.9
New railways of general use (kilometers)	1,616
Railway electrification (kilometers) .	2,313
Land irrigation (1000 hectares)	388
Land drainage (1000 hectares)	721

Besides, operating enterprises showed an increase in production capacities due to production mechanization and intensification, the improvement of production processes, plant modernization and other organization and technical measures. Steel smelting capacities grew by 2 million tons and ferrous rolled stock capacities by 400 thousand tons.

Among the biggest enterprises and projects made operational in 1965 are the following: the Plavinas and Kiev hydropower electric stations, twenty power generating units of 200,000-300,000 kw. at thermal power stations, the world's biggest blast furnace at the Zhdanov metallurgical works, the Korshunovo and Ingulets ore-concentration plants, the Navoi and Cherkassy chemical works, the Gomel super-phosphate plant and the first section of the second Soligorsk potash fertilizer works, the Kuibyshev and Dorogobuzh nitrogen fertilizer plants and the Kaunas artificial fibre factory.

The first production line of the huge Bratsk timber-processing complex became operational, and two big cement production lines were put into service at the Achinsk plant. The first sections of the Alma-Ata cotton mills and the Karaganda and Kutaisi footwear factories were built, a new weaving factory was constructed at the Dushanbe mills, staple silk factories were erected in the Perm region, etc.

In the field of the food industry, seven sugar refineries and some meat-packing plants were commissioned and a large number of milk, butter and cheese-making plants, canneries and mechanized bakeries were built. Big cold storage capacities were put into service in trade as well as in the food, meat and dairy and fish processing industries. The new railway Abakan-Taishet (over 700 km.) was put into regular service. Many other enterprises and projects were built.

In 1965 total capital investments in the national economy exceeded 48,000 million roubles, of which capital investments under the state plan accounted for 37,200 million roubles, or 7 per cent more than in 1964.

Contractor organizations fulfilled the plan by 99 percent and increased the volume of contractor work by 8 percent.

The plan for the growth of labor productivity in construction was fulfilled; the cost of construction and assembly work was somewhat reduced, and bigger profits were received than in 1964.

At the same time, there are still considerable shortcomings in construction. The annual plan for the commissioning of production capacities was underfulfilled in many branches. Individual construction projects still show the inadequate organization of work, the low quality of construction and finishing operations and the unsatisfactory utilization of construction machinery and mechanisms. A number of construction organizations did not cope with targets for growth of labor productivity and cost reduction; contractor organizations underfulfilled the plan for profits.

V. THE GROWTH OF THE LIVING AND CULTURAL STANDARDS OF THE PEOPLE

The average annual number of industrial, professional and office workers in the country was 76.9 million, and during the year increased by 3,600,000. The number of workers, engineers, technicians, and other specialists in industry, construction and agriculture increased by two million; the number of employees in transport, communications, trade and public catering enterprises increased by 600,000; the number of employees in schools, educational establishments, research, medical and preschool establishments increased by one million.

In 1965, as in previous years, there was no unemployment in the country.

In the past year vocational training schools trained about one million young skilled workers. About 14 million people have improved their qualifications and learned new trades by training individually and in teams and attending courses directly at industrial enterprises and collective farms.

At the end of 1964 and in 1965, wages were increased for 20 million workers in branches directly servicing the population. The pay for education workers was increased by an average of 26 per cent, for the health service workers by 24 per cent, for the municipal workers by 15 percent, and for the trade and public catering workers by 19 percent.

The minimum wage was raised for workers and employees in all branches of national economy which did not have such an increase of pay earlier.

State pensions for collective farmers were introduced at the beginning of last year. The number of pensioners receiving pensions from the Union centralized social insurance fund for collective farmers reached eight million by the end of the year.

All payments and grants received by the population from the social consumption funds in the shape of social insurance benefits, various subsidies, pensions, stipends, paid holidays, free education, free medical service, accommodation in sanatoriums or rest-homes free of charge or cut rates, the maintenance of kindergartens, day-nurseries, etc., amounted to 41,500 million roubles, which is 13 per cent more than in 1964.

The average monthly wages and salaries in the country increased from 90 roubles in 1964 to 95 roubles in 1965, i.e., by 5.8 per cent. With the addition of grants and benefits received from the public funds average wages and salaries increased from 121 roubles to 128 roubles a month.

By the end of the year the total sum of the population's deposits in the country's savings banks reached 18,700 million roubles, an increase of 19 per cent during the year.

The volume of retail goods turnover in state and co-operative trade increased from 95,300 million roubles in 1964 to 10,500 million roubles in 1965, i.e., by 10 per cent (in comparable prices). A total of 1,100 million roubles' worth of goods purchased from the collective farmers and accepted from collective farms for sale on commission was also sold. The annual plan for retail trade was carried out ahead of schedule.

The sale of goods (state and cooperative network) was as follows:

	1965 as percentage of 1964
Bakery products	101
Meat & meat products	113
Fish, herring & other fish products	104
Butter	105
Vegetable oil	100
Wholemilk products	116
Cheese	118
Eggs	137
Sugar	105
Confectionery	100
Tea	105
Potatoes	91
Other vegetables	100
Fruit	117
Citrus fruit	110
Cotton fabrics	99
Woollen fabrics	115
Silk fabrics	112
Linen fabrics	122
Clothes & underwear	113
Knitted garments	117
Hosiery	115
Leather footwear	110
Porcelain, faïence & glass tableware	107
Soap & detergents	102
Furniture	105
Refrigerators	149
Washing machines	122
Vacuum cleaners	115
Clocks & watches	111
Motorcycles & scooters	108
Bicycles & mopeds	106
Radio sets & radiograms	108
TV sets	126
Cameras	135
Cars	92

While trade turnover has risen considerably, public demand for some items of consumer goods is still not being fully satisfied; the plan for trade turnover of public catering was slightly unfulfilled.

State retail prices were lowered in the past year on woollen, silk and linen textiles, on clothing and underwear made out of these fabrics, and several other items of consumer goods; these price reductions saved the population more than 1,200 million roubles in one year.

In comparison with 1964, prices on collective farm markets dropped on the average by 6 percent, and sales went up.

Successes in the development of the national economy, and growth of retail trade turnover and services rendered to the population, secured, as in previous years, the stability of money circulation.

Further successes have been achieved in the fields of public education, science and culture.

More than 71 million people attended various educational establishments in the past year; 48 million studied in general educational schools of all kinds—1.6 million more than in 1964. More than 4 million finished eight-year schools, and 1.3 million graduated from secondary schools; extended-day schools and groups and boarding schools were attended by 3.4 million pupils.

The number of students in higher and special secondary schools is 7.5 million—3.8 million in higher schools, and 3.7 million in special secondary schools. In 1965 the country received one million specialists—400,000 with a higher education, and 600,000 with a special secondary education.

The total number of scientific workers engaged in research institutions, higher schools and other organizations exceeded 660,000 by the end of the year.

During the year, the number of cinema projectors increased by 6,000 and reached a total of 145,000. Cinema attendance totalled 4,300 million, increasing by 139 million in comparison with 1964.

Housing construction is being carried out on a large scale. About 78 million square metres of housing—nearly 3 million square metres more than in 1964—were turned over for occupancy in urban and rural communities at the expense of the state, of the population and with the aid of state credits. More than 6 million square metres were put up by house-building cooperatives, a 32 percent increase over last year. In addition, more than 350,000 homes were built on the collective farms (by the farms, farmers, and rural intelligentsia).

During last year alone, more than 10 million people moved into new apartments and homes or improved their living conditions in houses built earlier.

General educational schools for 1.8 million pupils, hospitals for more than 65,000 in-patients, and pre-school establishments for 540,000 children were built at the expense of the state and the collective farms.

However, the plan for delivering housing, and cultural and public service establishments was underfulfilled in the country as a whole and in many Republics.

Installation of gas in homes was carried on on an extensive scale. In the past year, the number of apartments that obtained gas increased by 1.6 million, or 19 percent.

Medical services for the population continued to improve. The number of doctors of all specialties rose in the past year by nearly 25,000. The number of beds in hospitals, sanatoriums, rest-homes and boarding-houses increased.

The population of the USSR was almost 232 million as of January 1, 1966.

CENTRAL STATISTICAL BOARD UNDER THE
USSR COUNCIL OF MINISTERS

Reading No. 35 — SOVIET INDUSTRIAL HIERARCHY, 1955 *

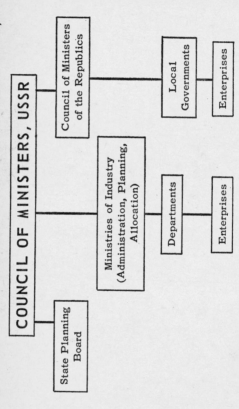

* Prepared by author.

Reading No. 36 — SOVIET INDUSTRIAL HIERARCHY, 1957 *

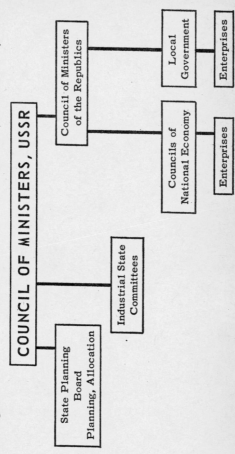

* Reading 36 and 36A prepared by author.

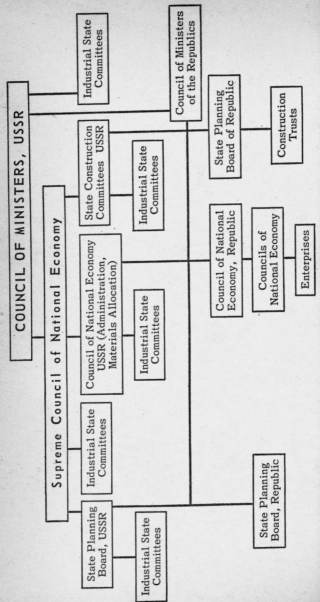

36A—Soviet Industrial Hierarchy, 1963

THE GAP BETWEEN KHRUSHCHEV AND KOSYGIN*

Item	Unit	1965 Actual	1970 Kosygin's target	1970 Khrushchev's target
Electric power	billion kw. hours	507	840-850	900-1,000
Crude steel	million tons	91	124-129	145
Crude oil	million tons	243	345-355	390
Natural gas	billion cubic metres	129	225-240	310-325
Cement	million tons	72	100-105	122
Mineral fertilizers	(in conventional units)	31	62-65	77
Synthetic tars and plastics	thousand tons	821	2,100-2,300	5,300
Man-made fibres	thousand tons	407	780-830	1,350

* From: *The Economist*, February 26, 1966. Page 782.

TRADE OF SOME NATO COUNTRIES WITH THE USSR, 1961-1963*

U.S. EXPORTS TO USSR
(Millions of dollars, f.o.b.)
1963

Cattle hides	6.3
Chemicals, except organic	4.3
Petroleum coke	4.0
Organic chemicals	3.9
Tallow, inedible	2.1
Total	20.6
Total exports	22.9

U.S. IMPORTS FROM USSR
(Millions of dollars, f.o.b.)
1963

Fur skins	6.8
Palladium	4.0
Chrome ore	3.7
Platinum	2.5
Rhodium	1.6
Total	18.6
Total imports	21.2

* Source withheld by request.

BRITISH EXPORTS TO USSR
(Millions of dollars, f.o.b.)
1963

Plates and sheets of iron and steel	30.8
Machinery, non-electric, except machines for special industries	28.6
Machines for special industries	26.0
Rubber, including synthetic and reclaimed	22.5
Chemicals	22.5
Manmade fibers, yarn and woven material	15.0
Iron and steel products, except sheets and plates	6.2
Machinery, electric	5.7
Tin and alloys, unwrought	4.7
Total	162.0
Total exports	178.8

BRITISH IMPORTS FROM USSR
(Millions of dollars, f.o.b.)
1963

	Million dollars
Wood in all shapes	100.2
Fur skins, undressed and dressed	34.9
Iron and steel coils for rerolling	20.9
Wheat	20.1
Plywood	12.4
Aluminum, lead, zinc & alloys, unwrought	9.5
Vegetable textile fibers	7.3
Pulp and waste paper	7.2
Sugar raw and refined	5.2
Chemicals	4.8
Fish and fish preparations	4.7
Petroleum products	3.7
Platinum and platinum group metals	3.0
Manganese ore and concentrates	2.9
Total	236.8
Total imports	254.7

FRENCH EXPORTS TO USSR
(Millions of dollars, f.o.b.)
1963

Machinery, non-electric, except thermal apparatus and pumps	11.6
Sheets and plates of iron and steel	8.2
Nickel unwrought, unalloyed	5.3
Thermal apparatus	5.3
Chemicals except essential oils & resinoids	5.1
Machinery, electric	4.6
Fibers & woven fabrics, manmade	4.6
Pumps	3.4
Essential oils & resinoids	2.9
Wheat flour	2.6
Paper and paperboard	1.8
Total	55.4
Total exports	64.2

FRENCH IMPORTS FROM USSR
(Millions of dollars, c.i.f.)
1963

Coal	46.4
Petroleum and petroleum products	26.9
Wood	21.7
Iron and steel coils for rerolling	6.4
Fur skins undressed, and furs dressed	5.9
Fish and fish preparations	5.2
Woodpulp, sulfate and sulfite	4.4
Platinum and alloys, unworked	4.3
Manganese & chromium ores and concentrates	3.4
Cotton	2.9
Feedingstuff for animals	2.6
Asbestos	2.3
Chemicals	2.0
Palladium & alloys, unworked	1.1
Total	135.5
Total imports	141.1

ITALIAN EXPORTS TO USSR
(Millions of dollars, f.o.b.)
1963

Machinery, non-electric, except metal-working machine tools	30.8
Chemicals	14.4
Iron and steel products, except high pressure conduits of steel	12.0
Manmade fibers and yarn	10.6
Machinery, electric	9.7
High pressure conduits of steel	8.3
Metalworking machine tools	5.9
Fruits and vegetables	5.5
Synthetic rubber and rubber substitutes	4.5
Total	101.7
Total exports	114.3

ITALIAN IMPORTS FROM USSR
(Millions of dollars, c.i.f.)
1963

	Million dollars
Petroleum, crude and partly refined	76.0
Coal	15.7
Wood in all shapes	12.9
Hematite and phosphorus pig iron	9.6
Petroleum products	9.4
Coils for rerolling or iron and steel	8.7
Corn and barley	7.2
Chemicals	5.9
Sugar	5.6
Blooms and billets or iron & steel, rolled	4.5
Cotton	4.1
Iron pyrites, unroasted	2.1
Total	161.7
Total imports	175.8

WEST GERMAN EXPORTS TO USSR
(Millions of dollars, f.o.b.)
1963

Machinery, non-electric, except machine tools and complete plant installation	29.6
Ships	21.7
Chemicals	19.0
Tubes and pipes of iron and steel	18.4
Complete plant installations	12.7
Sheets and plates of iron and steel	11.0
Metalcutting machine tools	7.6
Machinery, electric	7.6
Copper, refined, unalloyed	6.3
Wheat flour	6.1
Manmade fibers	2.8
Total	142.8
Total exports	153.6

WEST GERMAN IMPORTS FROM USSR
(Millions of dollars, c.i.f.)
1963

Petroleum crude and partly refined	27.8
Wood in all shapes	22.9
Fur skins, undressed	17.6
Petroleum products	14.9
Cotton	12.3
Wheat	9.4
Platinum and platinum group metals	6.4
Iron and steel coils for recolling	5.7
Sugar, refined and molasses	5.7
Manganese, chromium & tungsten ores and concentrates	4.8
Natural phosphates	4.6
Zinc, antimony, cadmium	3.2
Pig iron	2.9
Total	138.2
Total imports	163.7

A SELECTED BIBLIOGRAPHY

Baykov, A. *The Development of the Soviet Economic System*. Cambridge, Harvard University Press, 1946.

Bergson, A. *The Structure of Soviet Wages: A Study in Socialist Economics*. Harvard University Press, 1944.

Bienstock, G., A. Yugow, and S. Schwarz. *Management in Russian Industry and Agriculture*. New York, Oxford University Press, 1944.

Deutscher, I. *Soviet Trade Unions: Their Place in Soviet Labor Policy*. London, Royal Institute of International Affairs, 1950.

Dobb, M. *Soviet Economic Development Since 1917*. London, Routledge, 1948.

Erlich, Alexander. *The Soviet Industrialization Debate, 1924-1928*. Cambridge, Harvard University Press, 1960.

Gordon, M. *Russian Workers before and since Lenin*. New York, Dutton, 1941.

Hubbard, L. E. *The Economics of Soviet Agriculture*. New York, Macmillan, 1939.

Hubbard, L. E. *Soviet Labor and Industry*. London, Macmillan, 1942.

Jasny, N. *The Socialized Agriculture of the USSR*. Stanford, Stanford University Press, 1949.

Laird, Roy D. (ed.) *Soviet Agricultural and Peasant Affairs*. Slavic Series I. Un. of Kansas Press, Lawrence, 1963.

Liashchenko, Peter. *History of the National Economy of Russia to the 1917 Revolution*. N.Y., Macmillan, 1949.

Maynard, Sir John. *Russia in Flux*. N.Y., Macmillan, 1948.

Miller, M. *Economic Development of Russia, 1905-1914*. London, King, 1926.

Pavlovsky, G. *Agricultural Russia on the Eve of the Revolution*. London, Routledge, 1930.

The Road to Communism. Documents of the 22nd Congress of the Communist Party of the Soviet Union, Oct. 17-31, 1961. Moscow, Foreign Languages Publishing House, 1961.

Schwartz, H. *Russia's Soviet Economy*. New York, Prentice-Hall, 1954.

Schwartz, H. *The Soviet Economy since Stalin*. Philadelphia and New York, J. B. Lippincott Co., 1965.

The Soviet Seven Year Plan, 1959-1965. With a Foreword by A. W. Haslett. London, Todd Reference Books, 1959.

"The Soviet Union since World War II." *The Annals*, May 1949.

Stalin, J. *The Great Patriotic War of the Soviet Union.* New York, International Publishers, 1945.

Volin, L. *A Survey of Soviet Russian Agriculture.* Washington, U.S. Government Printing Office, 1951.

Yugow, A. *Russia's Economic Front for War and Peace:* An *Appraisal of the Three Five Year Plans.* New York, Harper, 1942.

INDEX

VAN NOSTRAND ANVIL BOOKS already published